Developmentally Appropriate Practice in Early Childhood Programs Serving Children From Birth Through Age 8

Expanded Edition

SUE BREDEKAMP, *Editor*

National Association for the Education of Young Children
1834 Connecticut Avenue, N.W., Washington, DC 20009-5786

The National Association for the Education of Young Children attempts through its publications program to provide a forum for discussion of major issues and ideas in our field. We hope to provoke thoughts and promote professional growth. The views expressed or implied are not necessarily those of the Association.

Copies of *Developmentally Appropriate Practice in Early Childhood Programs Serving Children From Birth Through Age 8* can be purchased from NAEYC, 1834 Connecticut Avenue, N.W., Washington, DC 20009-5786.

Library of Congress Catalog Number: 87-062626

ISBN Catalog Number: 0-935989-11-0

NAEYC #224

Printed in the United States of America.

Contents

Preface

When the first edition of this book was published in November 1986, it was quickly apparent that a major need had been addressed. In the next 10 months, 25,000 copies (and more than 85,000 copies of a brochure entitled "Good Teaching Practices for 4- and 5-Year-Olds") were distributed. The first edition included a broad statement describing developmentally appropriate practice across the full age span of early childhood—birth through age 8—and more detailed descriptions of appropriate and inappropriate practices for infants and toddlers and for 4- and 5-year-olds. These age groups were described in greater detail because they were the areas where the greatest need for clarification had been expressed. Several trends contributed to the need for these clear definitions of appropriate practice including the trend toward increased numbers of infants and toddlers in group care and the concern that kindergarten and even prekindergarten programs were becoming watered-down first grades with too much emphasis on teacher-directed instruction in narrowly defined academic skills.

Immediately, readers of the book's first edition informed NAEYC of other areas in need of clear descriptions of appropriate practice—programs serving 3-year-olds and primary grade schools. This expanded edition contains all the material from the first book plus new chapters on appropriate practices for 3-year-olds and for primary grades; successful transitions; and strategies to inform others about developmentally appropriate practice. These statements include descriptions of inappropriate as well as appropriate practices because people often learn what to do by learning what *not* to do. Sensitive readers will soon see that the younger the children are, the more inappropriate practices appear neglectful or border on abusive.

It was during the development of NAEYC's accreditation system, the National Academy of Early Childhood Programs, that the need for a clearer definition of developmentally appropriate practice first arose. Many of the accreditation Criteria refer to "developmentally appropriate activities ... materials ... or expectations." Without further information, these Criteria are subject to varying interpretations. Now that the accreditation system is operating, it has become even more important to have clear descriptions of the meaning of key terms and no concept is more key to defining quality than "developmental appropriateness."

This book represents the early childhood profession's consensus definition of developmentally appropriate practice in early childhood programs. It is intended for use by teachers, administrators, parents, policymakers, and others involved with programs serving young children, birth through age 8, in schools, centers, and homes. As with so many NAEYC projects, it represents the thoughtful suggestions and careful review of hundreds of early childhood professionals.

The concept of developmentally appropriate practice can be summarized, to use Hunt's phrase, as a problem of the match. What is perfectly acceptable for one age group is inappropriate for another because it does not match the child's developmental level. Just as acceptable elementary school practice is often inappropriate for preschoolers, many common preschool practices are inappropriate for toddlers. We shudder at those who would teach 4-year-olds like fourth graders, but we must also shake our heads when 18-month-olds are expected to function like 4-year-olds.

Development is a truly fascinating and wonderful phenomenon. It is not something to be accelerated or skipped. One period of childhood or aspect of development is not better or more important than another; each has its own tasks to accomplish. Hopefully, the descriptions of developmentally appropriate practice in this book will help adults who work with young children provide the best quality care and education for each child so that they in turn may develop to their fullest potential.

PART 1

NAEYC Position Statement on Developmentally Appropriate Practice in Early Childhood Programs Serving Children From Birth Through Age 8

Introduction

The quality of our nation's educational system has come under intense public scrutiny in the 1980s. While much of the attention has been directed at secondary and postsecondary education, the field of early childhood education must also examine its practices in light of current knowledge of child development and learning.

The purpose of this paper is to describe developmentally appropriate practice in early childhood programs for administrators, teachers, parents, policy makers, and others who make decisions about the care and education of young children. An early childhood program is any part-day or full-day group program in a center, school, or other facility that serves children from birth through age 8. Early childhood programs include child care centers, private and public preschools, kindergartens, and primary grade schools.

Rationale

In recent years, a trend toward increased emphasis on formal instruction in academic skills has emerged in early childhood programs. This trend toward formal academic instruction for younger children is based on misconceptions about early learning (Elkind, 1986). Despite the trend among some educators to formalize instruction, there has been no comparable evidence of change in what young children need for optimal development or how they learn. In fact, a growing body of research has emerged recently affirming that children learn most effectively through a concrete, play-oriented approach to early childhood education.

In addition to an increased emphasis on academics, early childhood programs have experienced other changes. The number of progams has increased in response to the growing demand for out-of-home care and education during the early years. Some characteristics of early childhood programs have also changed in the last few years. For example, children are now enrolled in programs at younger ages, many from infancy. The length of the program day for all ages of children has been extended in response to the need for extended hours of care for employed families. Similarly, program sponsorship has become more diverse. The public schools are playing a larger role in providing prekindergarten programs or before- and after-school child care. Corporate America is also becoming a more visible sponsor of child care programs.

Programs have changed in response to social, economic, and political forces; however, these changes have not always taken into account the basic developmental needs of young children, which have remained constant. The trend toward early academics, for example, is antithetical to what we know about how young children learn. Programs should be tailored to meet the needs of children, rather than expecting children to adjust to the demands of a specific program.

Position Statement

The National Association for the Education of Young Children (NAEYC) believes that a high quality early childhood program provides a safe and nurturing environment that promotes the physical, social, emotional, and cognitive development of young children while responding to the needs of families. Although the quality of an early childhood program may be affected by many factors, a major determinant of program quality is the extent to which knowledge of child development is applied in program practices—the degree to which the program is *developmentally appropriate.* NAEYC believes that high quality, developmentally appropriate programs should be available to all children and their families.

In this position paper, the concept of *developmental appropriateness* will first be defined. Then guidelines will be presented describing how developmental appropriateness can be applied to four components of early childhood programs: curriculum; adult-child interactions; relations between the home and program; and developmental evaluation of children. The statement concludes with a discussion of major policy implications and recommendations. These guidelines are designed to be used in conjunction with NAEYC's Criteria for High Quality Early Childhood Programs, the standards for accreditation by the National Academy of Early Childhood Programs (NAEYC, 1984).

Definition of developmental appropriateness

The concept of *developmental appropriateness* has two dimensions: age appropriateness and individual appropriateness.

1. **Age appropriateness.** Human development research indicates that there are universal, predictable sequences of growth and change that occur in children during the first 9 years of life. These predictable changes occur in all domains of development—physical, emotional, social, and cognitive. Knowledge of typical development of children within the age span served by the program provides a framework from which teachers prepare the learning environment and plan appropriate experiences.

2. **Individual appropriateness.** Each child is a unique person with an individual pattern and timing of growth, as well as individual personality, learning style, and family background. Both the curriculum and adults' interactions with children should be responsive to individual differences. Learning in young children is the result of interaction between the child's thoughts and experiences with materials, ideas, and people. These experiences should match the child's developing abilities, while also challenging the child's interest and understanding.

Teachers can use child development knowledge to identify the range of appropriate behaviors, activities, and materials for a specific age group. This knowledge

The curriculum and adults' interaction are responsive to individual differences in ability and interests.

Vivienne della Grotta

2

is used in conjunction with understanding about individual children's growth patterns, strengths, interests, and experiences to design the most appropriate learning environment. Although the content of the curriculum is determined by many factors such as tradition, the subject matter of the disciplines, social or cultural values, and parental desires, for the content and teaching strategies to be developmentally appropriate they must be age appropriate and individually appropriate.

Children's play is a primary vehicle for and indicator of their mental growth. Play enables children to progress along the developmental sequence from the sensorimotor intelligence of infancy to preoperational thought in the preschool years to the concrete operational thinking exhibited by primary children (Fein, 1979; Fromberg, 1986; Piaget, 1952; Sponseller, 1982). In addition to its role in cognitive development, play also serves important functions in children's physical, emotional, and social development (Herron & Sutton-Smith, 1974). Therefore, child-initiated, child-directed, teacher-supported play is an essential component of developmentally appropriate practice (Fein & Rivkin, 1986).

Guidelines for Developmentally Appropriate Practice

I. Curriculum

A developmentally appropriate curriculum for young children is planned to be appropriate for the age span of the children within the group and is implemented with attention to the different needs, interests, and developmental levels of those individual children.

A. Developmentally appropriate curriculum provides for all areas of a child's development: physical, emotional, social, and cognitive through an integrated approach (Almy, 1975; Biber, 1984; Elkind, 1986; Forman & Kuschner, 1983; Kline, 1985; Skeen, Garner, & Cartwright, 1984; Spodek, 1985).

Realistic curriculum goals for children should address all of these areas in age-appropriate ways. Children's learning does not occur in narrowly defined subject areas; their development and learning are integrated. Any activity that stimulates one dimension of development and learning affects other dimensions as well.

B. Appropriate curriculum planning is based on teachers' observations and recordings of each child's special interests and developmental progress (Almy, 1975; Biber, 1984; Cohen, Stern, & Balaban, 1983; Goodwin & Goodwin, 1982).

Realistic curriculum goals and plans are based on regular assessment of individual needs, strengths, and interests. Curriculum is based on both age-appropriate and individually appropriate information. For example, individual children's family/cultural backgrounds—such as expressive styles, ways of interacting, play, and games—are used to broaden the curriculum for all children.

C. Curriculum planning emphasizes learning as an interactive process. Teachers prepare the environment for children to learn through active exploration and interaction with adults, other children, and materials (Biber, 1984; Fein, 1979; Forman & Kuschner, 1983; Fromberg, 1986; Goffin & Tull, 1985; Griffin, 1982; Kamii, 1985; Lay-Dopyera & Dopyera, 1986; Powell, 1986; Sponseller, 1982).

The process of interacting with materials and people results in learning. Finished products or "correct" solutions that conform to adult standards are not very accurate criteria for judging whether learning has occurred. Much of young children's learning takes place when they direct their own play activities. During play, children feel successful when they engage in a task they have defined for themselves, such as finding their way through an obstacle course with a friend or pouring water into and out of various containers. Such learning should not be inhibited by adult-established concepts of completion, achievement, and failure. Activities should be designed to concentrate on furthering emerging skills through creative activity and intense involvement.

D. Learning activities and materials should be concrete, real, and relevant to the lives of young children (Almy, 1975; Biber, 1984; Evans, 1984; Forman & Kuschner, 1983; Hawkins, 1970; Hirsch, 1984; Holt, 1979; Kamii, 1985; Kline, 1985; Piaget, 1972; Schickedanz, 1986; Seefeldt, 1986; Smith, 1985; Weber, 1984).

Children need years of play with real objects and events before they are able to understand the meaning of symbols such as letters and numbers. Learning takes place as young children touch, manipulate, and experiment with things and interact with people. Throughout early childhood, children's concepts and language gradually develop to enable them to understand more abstract or symbolic information. Pictures and stories should be used frequently to build upon children's real experiences.

Workbooks, worksheets, coloring books, and adult-made models of art products for children to copy are *not* appropriate for young children, especially those younger than 6. Children older than 5 show increasing abilities to learn through written exercises, oral presentations, and other adult-directed teaching strategies.

Child-initiated, child-directed, teacher-supported play is an essential component of developmentally appropriate practice.

Subjects & Predicates

However, the child's active participation in self-directed play with concrete, real-life experiences continues to be a key to motivated, meaningful learning in kindergarten and the primary grades.

Basic learning materials and activities for an appropriate curriculum include sand, water, clay, and accessories to use with them; hollow, table, and unit blocks; puzzles with varying numbers of pieces; many types of games; a variety of small manipulative toys; dramatic play props such as those for housekeeping and transportation; a variety of science investigation equipment and items to explore; a changing selection of appropriate and aesthetically pleasing books and recordings; supplies of paper, water-based paint and markers, and other materials for creative expression; large muscle equipment; field trips; classroom responsibilities, such as helping with routines; and positive interactions and problem-solving opportunities with other children and adults.

E. Programs provide for a wider range of developmental interests and abilities than the chronological age range of the group would suggest. Adults are prepared to meet the needs of children who exhibit unusual interests and skills outside the normal developmental range (Kitano, 1982; Languis, Sanders, & Tipps, 1980; Schickedanz, Schickedanz, & Forsyth, 1982; Souweine, Crimmins, & Mazel, 1981; Uphoff & Gilmore, 1985).

Activities and equipment should be provided for a chronological age range which in many cases is at least 12 months. However, the normal developmental age range in any group may be as much as 2 years. Some mainstreamed situations will demand a wider range of expectations. When the developmental age range of a group is more than 18 months, the need increases for a large variety of furnishings, equipment, and teaching strategies. The complexity of materials should also reflect the age span of the group. For example, a group that includes 3-, 4-, and 5-year-olds would need books of varying length and complexity; puzzles with varying numbers and sizes of pieces; games that require a range of skills and abilities to follow rules; and other diverse materials, teaching methods, and room arrangements.

F. Teachers provide a variety of activities and materials; teachers increase the difficulty, complexity, and challenge of an activity as children are involved with it and as children develop understanding and skills (Davidson, 1985; Ferreiro & Teberosky, 1982; Forman & Kaden, 1986; Gerber, 1982; Gilbert, 1981; Gonzalez-Mena & Eyer, 1980; Greenberg, 1976; Hill, 1979; Hirsch, 1984; Holt, 1979; Honig, 1980, 1981; Kamii, 1982, 1985; Kamii & DeVries, 1980; Lasky & Mukerji, 1980; McDonald, 1979; National Institute of Education, 1984; Schickedanz, 1986; Smith, 1982; Smith, 1983; Sparling, 1984; Stewart, 1982; Veach, 1977; Willert & Kamii, 1985; Willis & Ricciuti, 1975).

As children work with materials or activities, teachers listen, observe, and interpret children's behavior. Teachers can then facilitate children's involvement and learning by asking questions, making suggestions, or adding more complex materials or ideas to a situation. During a program year, as well as from one year to another, activities and environments

Learning activities and materials should be concrete, real, and relevant to the lives of young children.

Carolyn Williams

for children should change in arrangement and inventory, and special events should also be planned. Examples of developmentally appropriate learning activities for various age groups follow.

1. Infants and toddlers

Infants and toddlers learn by experiencing the environment through their senses (seeing, hearing, tasting, smelling, and feeling), by physically moving around, and through social interaction. Nonmobile infants absorb and organize a great deal of information about the world around them, so adults talk and sing with them about what is happening and bring them objects to observe and manipulate. At times adults carry nonmobile infants around the environment to show them interesting events and people. Mobile infants and toddlers increasingly use toys, language, and other learning materials in their play.

Adults play a vital socialization role with infants and toddlers. Warm, positive relationships with adults help infants develop a sense of trust in the world and feelings of competence. These interactions are critical for the development of the children's healthy self-esteem. The trusted adult becomes the secure base from which the mobile infant or toddler explores the environment.

Important independence skills are being acquired during these years, including personal care such as toileting, feeding, and dressing. The most appropriate teaching technique for this age group is to give ample opportunities for the children to use self-initiated repetition to practice newly acquired skills and to experience feelings of autonomy and success. Infants will bat at, grasp, bang, or drop their toys. Patience is essential as a toddler struggles to put on a sweater. Imitation, hiding, and naming games are also important for learning at this age. Realistic toys will enable children to engage in increasingly complex types of play.

Two-year-olds are learning to produce language rapidly. They need simple books, pictures, puzzles, and music, and time and space for active play such as jumping, running, and dancing. Toddlers are acquiring

Infants and toddlers learn by experiencing the environment through their senses.

David Phillips

social skills, but in groups there should be several of the same toy because egocentric toddlers are not yet able to understand the concept of sharing.

2. Three-, 4-, and 5-year-olds

Curriculum for 3-year-olds should emphasize language, activity, and movement, with major emphasis on large muscle activity. Appropriate activities include dramatic play, wheel toys and climbers, puzzles and blocks, and opportunities to talk and listen to simple stories.

Four-year-olds enjoy a greater variety of experiences and more small motor activities like scissors, art, manipulatives, and cooking. They are more able to concentrate and remember as well as recognize objects by shape, color, or size. Four-year-olds are developing basic math concepts and problem-solving skills.

Some 4-year-olds and most 5-year-olds combine ideas into more complex relations (for example, number concepts such as one-to-one correspondence) and have growing memory capacity and fine motor physical skills. Some 4-year-olds and most 5s display a growing interest in the functional aspects of written language, such as recognizing meaningful words and trying to write their own names. Activities designed solely to teach the alphabet, phonics, and penmanship are much less appropriate for this age group than providing a print-rich environment that stimulates the development of language and literacy skills in a meaningful context.

Curriculum for 4s and 5s can expand beyond the child's immediate experience of self, home, and family to include special events and trips. Five-year-olds are developing interest in community and the world outside their own. They also use motor skills well, even daringly, and show increasing ability to pay attention for longer times and in larger groups if the topic is meaningful.

3. Six-, 7-, and 8-year-olds

Six-year-olds are active and demonstrate considerable verbal ability; they are becoming interested in games and rules and develop concepts and problem-solving skills from these experiences. Most 6-year-olds and many 7- and 8-year-olds may be more mature mentally than physically. Therefore, hands-on activity and experimentation is more appropriate for this age group than fatiguing mechanical seatwork.

Seven-year-olds seem to need time to catch up and practice with many newly acquired physical and cognitive skills. They become increasingly able to reason, to listen to others, and to show social give-and-take.

Eight-year-olds combine great curiosity with increased social interest. Now they are able to learn about other, more distant peoples. During first, second, and third grade, children can learn from the symbolic experiences of reading books and listening to stories; however, their understanding of what they read is based on their ability to relate the written word to their own experience. Primary grade children also learn to communicate through written language, dictating or writing stories about their own experiences or fantasies. The same is true of the development of number concepts. Children's mathematical concepts develop from their own thinking during games and real-life experiences that involve quantification, such as cooking or carpentry.

Teachers increase the difficulty, complexity, and challenge of an activity as children are involved with it and as children develop understanding and skills.

Marietta Lynch

G. Adults provide opportunities for children to choose from among a variety of activities, materials, and equipment; and time to explore through active involvement. Adults facilitate children's engagement with materials and activities and extend the child's learning by asking questions or making suggestions that stimulate children's thinking (Elkind, 1986; Forman & Kuschner, 1983; Goffin & Tull, 1985; Kamii & Lee-Katz, 1979; Lay-Dopyera & Dopyera, 1986; Sackoff & Hart, 1984; Skeen, Garner, & Cartwright, 1984; Sparling, 1984).

Children of all ages need uninterrupted periods of time to become involved, investigate, select, and persist at activities. The teacher's role in child-chosen activity is to prepare the environment with stimulating, challenging activity choices and then to facilitate children's engagement. In developmentally appropriate programs, adults:

1. provide a rich variety of activities and materials from which to choose.

   Such variety increases the likelihood of a child's prolonged or satisfied attention and increases independence and opportunity for making decisions.

2. offer children the choice to participate in a small group or in a solitary activity.

3. assist and guide children who are not yet able to use easily and enjoy child-choice activity periods.

4. provide opportunities for child-initiated, child-directed practice of skills as a self-chosen activity.

   Children need opportunities to repeat acquired skills to fully assimilate their learning. Repetition that is initiated and directed by the child, not adult-directed drill and practice, is most valuable for assimilation.

H. Multicultural and nonsexist experiences, materials, and equipment should be provided for children of all ages (Ramsey, 1979, 1982; Saracho & Spodek, 1983; Sprung, 1978).

Providing a wide variety of multicultural, nonstereotyping materials and activities helps ensure the individual appropriateness of the curriculum and also

1. enhances each child's self-concept and esteem,

2. supports the integrity of the child's family,

3. enhances the child's learning processes in both the home and the early childhood program by strengthening ties,

4. extends experiences of children and their families to include knowledge of the ways of others, especially those who share the community, and

5. enriches the lives of all participants with respectful acceptance and appreciation of differences and similarities among them.

Multicultural experiences should not be limited to a celebration of holidays and should include foods, music, families, shelter, and other aspects common to all cultures.

Multicultural experiences should not be limited to a celebration of holidays and should include foods, music, families, shelter, and other aspects common to all cultures.

Nya Kwiawon Taryor

I. Adults provide a balance of rest and active movement for children throughout the program day (Cratty, 1982; Curtis, 1986; Hendrick, 1986; Stewart, 1982; Willis & Ricciuti, 1975).

For infants and toddlers, naps and quiet activities such as listening to rhymes and music provide periodic rest from the intense physical exploration that is characteristic of this age group. Two-year-olds, and many 3s, will need morning and/or afternoon naps, and should also have periods of carefully planned transition to quieting-down or rousing, especially before and after eating and sleeping. Children at about 2½- to 3-years-old become able to maintain brief interest in occasional small-group, teacher-conducted activities, and may enjoy quiet stories, music, and fingerplays together between periods of intense activity. Most 4s and many 5s still need naps, especially if their waking days are very long as they are in some child care situations. Children at this age need planned alternations of active and quiet activities and are usually willing to participate in brief, interesting, small-group activities. Older children continue to need alternating periods of active and quiet activity throughout the day, beyond traditionally provided recess.

The pace of the program day will vary depending on the length of time children are present, but children should never be rushed and schedules should be flexible enough to take advantage of impromptu experiences. The balance between active and quiet activity should be maintained throughout the day by alternating activities.

J. Outdoor experiences should be provided for children of all ages (Cratty, 1982; Curtis, 1986; Frost & Klein, 1979).

Because their physical development is occurring so rapidly, young children through age 8 need daily outdoor experiences to practice large muscle skills, learn about outdoor environments, and experience freedom not always possible indoors. Outdoor time is an integral part of the curriculum and requires planning; it is not simply a time for children to release pent-up energy.

Children should never be rushed and schedules should be flexible enough to take advantage of impromptu experiences. The balance between active and quiet activity should be maintained throughout the day.

II. Adult-Child Interaction

The developmental appropriateness of an early childhood program is most apparent in the interactions between adults and children. Developmentally appropriate interactions are based on adults' knowledge and expectations of age-appropriate behavior in children balanced by adults' awareness of individual differences among children.

A. **Adults respond quickly and directly to children's needs, desires, and messages and adapt their responses to children's differing styles and abilities** (Bell & Ainsworth, 1972; Erikson, 1950; Genishi, 1986; Greenspan & Greenspan, 1985; Honig, 1980, 1981; Lozoff, Brillenham, Trause, Kennell, & Klaus, 1977; Shure & Spivak, 1978; Smith & Davis, 1976).

Appropriate responses vary with the age of the child. Adults should respond immediately to infants' cries of distress. The response should be warm and soothing as the adult identifies the child's needs. Adults should also respond appropriately to infants' vocalizations, manipulation of objects, and movement, as these are the ways infants communicate. Adults hold and touch infants frequently; talk and sing to infants in a soothing, friendly voice; smile and maintain eye contact with infants. For toddlers and 2-year-olds, adults remain close by, giving attention and physical comfort as needed. Adults repeat children's words, paraphrase, or use synonyms or actions to help assure toddlers that they are understood. As children get older, adult responses are characterized by less physical communication and more verbal responsiveness, although immediacy is still important. Positive responses such as smiles and interest, and concentrated attention on children's activity, are important. Adults move quietly and circulate among individuals in groups to communicate with children in a friendly and relaxed manner.

The developmental appropriateness of an early childhood program is most apparent in the interactions between adults and children.

From infancy through the primary grades, adult communication with children is facilitated by sitting low or kneeling, and making eye contact. With all age groups, adults should also be aware of the powerful influence of modeling and other nonverbal communication; adults' actions should be compatible with their verbal messages and confirm that children understand their messages.

B. Adults provide many varied opportunities for children to communicate (Cazden, 1981; Genishi, 1986; Gordon, 1970, 1975; Greenspan & Greenspan, 1985; Lay-Dopyera & Dopyera, 1986; McAfee, 1985; Schachter & Strage, 1982; Schickedanz, 1986.

Children acquire communication skills through hearing and using language, and as adults listen and respond to what children say. Communication skills grow out of the desire to use language to express needs, insights, and excitement, and to solve problems. Children do not learn language, or any other concepts, by being quiet and listening to a lecture from an adult. Listening experiences—when there is something meaningful to listen to such as a story or poetry—can enrich language learning. Most language interaction with infants and toddlers is on an individual basis, although occasionally a group of two or three children may gather to hear an absorbing story. Throughout the preschool years, individual abilities to sit and pay attention will vary considerably, but time periods are short and groups should be small. During kindergarten and the primary grades, children can listen to directions or stories for longer periods of time (gradually expanding as children get older). Individual and small group interactions are still the most effective because children have the opportunity for two-way communication with adults and other children. Total group instructional techniques are *not* as effective in facilitating the development of communication skills and other learning in young children.

Equally important are opportunities for children to engage in two-way communication with others. Infants use crying and body movements to communicate. Adult responses to this communication, including the use of soothing language and descriptions of what is happening, build the foundation for children's ability to use language and their ability to feel good about themselves. Children rapidly expand their ability to understand language in their early years, and from about the age of 2, children can engage in increasingly interesting and lengthy conversations with adults and other children. These one-on-one exchanges are critical throughout the early years. Children's questions, and their responses to questions, particularly open-ended questions, provide valuable information about the individual's level of thinking.

C. Adults facilitate a child's successful completion of tasks by providing support, focused attention, physical proximity, and verbal encouragement. Adults recognize that children learn from trial and error and that children's misconceptions reflect their developing thoughts (Cohen, Stern, & Balaban, 1983; Elkind, 1986; Gottfried, 1983; Kamii, 1985; Piaget, 1950; Veach, 1977; Wallinga & Sweaney, 1985; Wellman, 1982; Zavitkovsky, Baker, Berlfein, & Almy, 1986).

Real successes are important incentives for people of all ages to continue learning and maintain motivation. Children learn from their own mistakes. Adults can examine the problem with the child and, if appropriate, encourage the child to try again or to find alternatives. Teachers plan many open-ended activities that have more than one right answer, and value the unique responses of individual children.

D. Teachers are alert to signs of undue stress in children's behavior, and aware of appropriate stress-reducing activities and techniques (Dreikurs, Grunwald, & Pepper, 1982; Elkind, 1986; Gazda, 1973; Honig, 1986; McCracken, 1986; Warren, 1977).

Formal, inappropriate instructional techniques are a source of stress for young children. When children exhibit stress-related behavior, teachers should examine the program to ensure that expectations are appropriate and not placing excessive demands on children.

When children experience stress from other sources, adults can find ways to reduce or eliminate the problem, or help children cope with it. Appropriate adult behaviors may include cuddling and soothing a crying infant; offering a toddler a favorite toy; providing books, water play, body movement, music, and quiet times for older children; and physically comforting and listening to the concerns of a child of any age who is in distress. Children's responses to stress are as individual as their learning styles. An understanding adult who is sensitive to individual children's reactions is the key to providing appropriate comfort.

E. **Adults facilitate the development of self-esteem by respecting, accepting, and comforting children, regardless of the child's behavior** (Coopersmith, 1975; Gordon, 1970, 1975; Greenspan & Greenspan, 1985; Kobak, 1979; Kuczynski, 1983; Lickona, 1983; Moore, 1982; Mussen & Eisenberg-Bert, 1977; Riley, 1984; Rubin & Everett, 1982; Smith & Davis, 1976; Stone, 1978).

Understanding behavior that is not unusual for young children, such as messiness, interest in body parts and genital differences, crying and resistance, aggression, and later infraction of rules and truth, is the basis for appropriate guidance of young children. Developmentally appropriate guidance demonstrates respect for children. It helps them understand and grow, and is directed toward helping children develop self-control and the ability to make better decisions in the future.

Adult behaviors that are *never* acceptable toward children include: screaming in anger; neglect; inflicting physical or emotional pain; criticism of a child's person or family by ridiculing, blaming, teasing, insulting, name-calling, threatening, or using frightening or humiliating punishment. Adults should not laugh at children's behavior, nor discuss it among themselves in the presence of children.

F. **Adults facilitate the development of self-control in children** (Asher, Renshaw, & Hymel, 1982; Hoffman, 1975; Honig, 1985; Kopp, 1982; Lytton, 1979; Miller, 1984; Moore, 1982; Read, Gardner, & Mahler, 1986; Rogers & Ross, 1986; Schaffer, 1984; Stone, 1978; Wolfgang & Glickman, 1980; Yarrow, Scott, & Waxler, 1973; Yarrow & Waxler, 1976).

Children learn self-control when adults treat

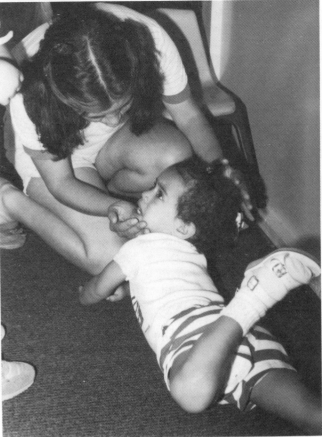

Subjects & Predicates

Developmentally appropriate guidance demonstrates respect for children. It helps them understand and grow and is directed toward helping children develop self-control and the ability to make better decisions in the future.

them with dignity and use discipline techniques such as

1. guiding children by setting clear, consistent, fair limits for classroom behavior; or in the case of older children, helping them to set their own limits;

2. valuing mistakes as learning opportunities;

3. redirecting children to more acceptable behavior or activity;

4. listening when children talk about their feelings and frustrations;

5. guiding children to resolve conflicts and modeling skills that help children to solve their own problems; and

6. patiently reminding children of rules and their rationale as needed.

11

G. Adults are responsible for all children under their supervision at all times and plan for increasing independence as children acquire skills (Stewart, 1982; Veach, 1977).

Adults must constantly and closely supervise and attend every child younger than the age of 3. They must be close enough to touch infants when awake, catch a climbing toddler before she hits the ground, be aware of every move of a 2-year-old, and be close enough to offer another toy when 2-year-olds have difficulty sharing. Adults must be responsible for 3- to 5-year-old children at all times, in an environment sufficiently open to permit it. Children older than 5 may be deemed, on individual bases, mature enough to leave the classroom or run independent errands within a building. This should happen only with the adult's permission and specific knowledge.

Children in all early childhood settings must be protected from unauthorized (by the guardian/family) adults and older children. Parents should be welcome visitors in the program, but provisions should be made for limited access to buildings, careful and close supervision of outdoor play areas, and policies which demand that visiting adults check with the administrative office before entering the children's areas. Constant adult vigilance is required with children birth through age 8 years. Young children should not be given the burden of protecting themselves from adults.

III. Relations Between the Home and Program

To achieve individually appropriate programs for young children, early childhood teachers must work in partnership with families and communicate regularly with children's parents.

A. Parents have both the right and the responsibility to share in decisions about their children's care and education. Parents should be encouraged to observe and participate. Teachers are responsible for establishing and maintaining frequent contacts with families (Brazelton, 1984; Croft, 1979; Dittmann, 1984; Honig, 1982; Katz, 1980; Lightfoot, 1978; Moore, 1982; Weissbourd, 1981).

During early childhood, children are largely dependent on their families for identity, security, care, and a general sense of well-being. Communication between families and teachers helps build mutual understanding and guidance, and provides greater consistency for children. Joint planning between families and teachers facilitates major socialization processes, such as toilet learning, developing peer relationships, and entering school.

B. Teachers share child development knowledge, insights, and resources as part of regular communication and conferences with family members (Brazelton, 1984; Croft, 1979; Dittmann, 1984; Lightfoot, 1978).

Mutual sharing of information and insights about the individual child's needs and developmental strides help both the family and the program. Regular communication and understanding about child development form a basis for mutual problem solving about concerns regarding behavior and growth. Teachers seek information from parents about individual children. Teachers promote mutual respect by recognizing and acknowledging different points of view to help minimize confusion for children.

C. Teachers, parents, agencies, programs, and consultants who may have educational responsibility for the child at different times should, with family participation, share developmental information about children as they pass from one level or program to another (Lightfoot, 1978; Meisels, 1985; Read, Gardner, & Mahler, 1986; Ziegler, 1985).

Continuity of educational experience is critical to supporting development. Such continuity results from communication both horizontally, as children change programs within a given year, and vertically, as children move on to other settings.

IV. Developmental Evaluation of Children

Assessment of individual children's development and learning is essential for planning and implementing developmentally appropriate programs, but should be used with caution to prevent discrimination against individuals and to ensure accuracy. Accurate testing can only be achieved with reliable, valid instruments and such instruments developed for use with young children are extremely rare. In the absence of valid instruments, testing is not valuable. Therefore, assessment of young children should rely heavily on the results of observations of their development and descriptive data.

A. Decisions that have a major impact on children such as enrollment, retention, or placement are not made on the basis of a single developmental assessment or screening device but consider other relevant information, particularly observations by teachers and parents. Developmental assessment of children's progress and achievements is used to adapt curriculum to match the developmental needs of children, to communicate with the child's family, and to evaluate the program's effectiveness (Cohen, Stern, & Balaban, 1983; Goodwin & Goodwin, 1982; Meisels, 1985; Standards for Educational and Psychological Testing, 1985; Uphoff & Gilmore, 1985).

Children acquire knowledge about the physical and social worlds in which they live through playful interaction with objects and people.

Scores on psychometric tests that measure narrowly defined academic skills should never be the sole criterion for recommending enrollment or retention in a program, or placement in special or remedial classes. Likewise, assessment of children should be used to evaluate the effectiveness of the curriculum, but the performance of children on standardized tests should not determine curriculum decisions.

B. Developmental assessments and observations are used to identify children who have special needs and/or who are at risk and to plan appropriate curriculum for them (Meisels, 1985).

This information is used to provide appropriate programming for these children and may be used in making professional referrals to families.

C. Developmental expectations based on standardized measurements and norms should compare any child or group of children only to normative information that is not only age-matched, but also gender-, culture-, and socioeconomically appropriate (Meisels, 1985; Standards for Educational and Psychological Testing, 1985; Uphoff & Gilmore, 1985).

The validity of comparative data analysis is questionable in the absence of such considerations.

D. In public schools, there should be a developmentally appropriate placement for every child of legal entry age.

No public school program should deny access to children of legal entry age on the basis of lack of maturational "readiness." For example, a kindergarten program that denies access to many 5-year-olds is not meeting the needs of its clients. Curriculum should be planned for the developmental levels of children and emphasize individual planning to address a wide range of developmental levels in a single classroom. It is the responsibility of the educational system to adjust to the developmental needs and levels of the children it serves; children should not be expected to adapt to an inappropriate system.

Policies Essential for Achieving Developmentally Appropriate Early Childhood Programs

The following policies are essential to implement NAEYC's Guidelines for Developmentally Appropriate Practice in Early Childhood Programs Serving Children From Birth Through Age 8. NAEYC strongly recommends that policy-making groups at the state and local levels consider the following when implementing early childhood programs.

A. Early childhood teachers should have college-level specialized preparation in early childhood education/child development. Teachers in early childhood programs, regardless of credentialed status, should be encouraged and supported to obtain and maintain current knowledge of child development and its application to early childhood educational practice (Almy, 1982; Feeney & Chun, 1985; NAEYC, 1982, 1985; Ruopp, Travers, Glantz, & Coelen, 1979).

Teachers must be knowledgeable about child development before they can implement a program based on child development principles. Implementing a developmentally appropriate program also requires preparation that is specifically designed for teaching young children through an individualized, concrete, experiential approach. Such preparation includes a foundation in theory and research of child development from birth through age 8, developmentally appropriate instructional methods, and field experiences.

B. Early childhood teachers should have practical experience teaching the age group. Therefore, regardless of credentialed status, teachers who have not previously taught young children should have supervised experience with young children before they can be in charge of a group (NAEYC, 1982, 1984).

C. Implementation of developmentally appropriate early childhood programs requires limiting the size of the group and providing sufficient numbers of adults to provide individualized and age-appropriate care and education (NAEYC, 1985; Ruopp, Travers, Glantz, & Coelen, 1979).

Even the most well-qualified teacher cannot individualize instruction and adequately supervise too large a group of young children. An acceptable adult-child ratio for 4- and 5-year-olds is 2 adults with no more than 20 children. Younger children require much smaller groups. Group size, and thus ratio of children to adults, should increase gradually through the primary grades.

References

These references include both laboratory and clinical classroom research to document the broad-based literature that forms the foundation for sound practice in early childhood education.

Almy, M. (1975). *The early childhood educator at work.* New York: McGraw-Hill.

Almy, M. (1982). Day care and early childhood education. In E. Zigler & E. Gordon (Eds.), *Daycare: Scientific and social policy issues* (pp. 476–495). Boston: Auburn House.

Asher, S.R., Renshaw, P.D., & Hymel, S. (1982). Peer relations and the development of social skills. In S. G. Moore & C.R. Cooper (Eds.), *The young child: Reviews of research* (Vol. 3, pp. 137–158). Washington, DC: NAEYC.

Bell, S., & Ainsworth, M.D.S. (1972). Infant crying and maternal responsiveness. *Child Development, 43,* 1171–1190.

Biber, B. (1984). *Early education and psychological development.* New Haven: Yale University Press.

Brazelton, T.B. (1984). Cementing family relationships through child care. In L. Dittman (Ed.), *The infants we care for* (rev. ed.) (pp. 9–20). Washington, DC: NAEYC.

Cazden, C. (Ed.). (1981). *Language in early childhood education* (rev. ed.). Washington, DC: NAEYC.

Cohen, D.H., Stern, V., & Balaban, N. (1983). *Observing and recording the behavior of young children* (3rd ed.). New York: Teachers College Press, Columbia University.

Coopersmith, S. (1975). Building self-esteem in the classroom. In S. Coopersmith (Ed.), *Developing motivation in young children.* San Francisco: Albion.

Cratty, B. (1982). Motor development in early childhood: Critical issues for researchers in the 1980s. In B. Spodek (Ed.), *Handbook of research in early childhood education.* New York: Free Press.

Croft, D. J. (1979). *Parents and teachers: A resource book for home, school, and community relations.* Belmont, CA: Wadsworth.

Curtis, S. (1986). New views on movement development and implications for curriculum in early childhood education. In C. Seefeldt (Ed.), *Early childhood curriculum: A review of current research.* New York: Teachers College Press, Columbia University.

Davidson, L. (1985). Preschool children's tonal knowledge: Antecedents of scale. In J. Boswell (Ed.), *The young child and music: Contemporary principles in child development and music education. Proceedings of the Music in Early Childhood Conference* (pp. 25–40). Reston, VA: Music Educators National Conference.

Dittmann, L. (1984). *The infants we care for.* Washington, DC: NAEYC.

Dreikurs, R., Grunwald, B., & Pepper, S. (1982). *Maintaining sanity in the classroom.* New York: Harper & Row.

Elkind, D. (1986, May). Formal education and early childhood education: An essential difference. *Phi Delta Kappan,* 631–636.

Erikson, E. (1950). *Childhood and society.* New York: Norton.

Evans, E. D. (1984). Children's aesthetics. In L. G. Katz (Ed.), *Current topics in early childhood education* (Vol. 5, pp. 73–104). Norwood, NJ: Ablex.

Feeney, S., & Chun, R. (1985). Research in review. Effective teachers of young children. *Young Children, 41*(1), 47–52.

Fein, G. (1979). Play and the acquisition of symbols. In L. Katz (Ed.), *Current topics in early childhood education* (Vol. 2). Norwood, NJ: Ablex.

Fein, G., & Rivkin, M. (Eds.). (1986). *The young child at play: Reviews of research* (Vol. 4). Washington, DC: NAEYC.

Ferreiro, E., & Teberosky, A. (1982). *Literacy before schooling.* Exeter, NH: Heinemann.

Forman, G., & Kaden, M. (1986). Research on science education in young children. In C. Seefeldt (Ed.), *Early childhood curriculum: A review of current research.* New York: Teachers College Press, Columbia University.

Forman, G., & Kuschner, D. (1983). *The child's construction of knowledge: Piaget for teaching children.* Washington, DC: NAEYC.

Fromberg, D. (1986). Play. In C. Seefeldt (Ed.), *Early childhood curriculum: A review of current research.* New York: Teachers College Press, Columbia University.

Frost, J. L., & Klein, B. L. (1979). *Children's play and playgrounds.* Austin, TX: Playgrounds International.

Gazda, G. M. (1973). *Human relations development: A manual for educators.* Boston: Allyn & Bacon.

Genishi, C. (1986). Acquiring language and communicative competence. In C. Seefeldt (Ed.), *Early childhood curriculum: A review of current research.* New York: Teachers College Press, Columbia University.

Gerber, M. (1982). What is appropriate curriculum for infants and toddlers? In B. Weissbourd & J. Musick (Eds.), *Infants: Their social environments.* Washington, DC: NAEYC.

Gilbert, J. P. (1981). Motoric music skill development in young children: A longitudinal investigation. *Psychology of Music, 9*(1), 21–24.

Goffin, S., & Tull, C. (1985). Problem solving: Encouraging active learning. *Young Children, 40*(3), 28–32.

Gonzalez-Mena, J., & Eyer, D. W. (1980). *Infancy and caregiving.* Palo Alto, CA: Mayfield.

Goodwin, W., & Goodwin, L. (1982). Measuring young children. In B. Spodek (Ed.), *Handbook of research in early childhood education.* New York: Free Press.

Gordon, T. (1970). *Parent effectiveness training.* New York: Wyden.

Gordon, T. (1975). *Teacher effectiveness training.* New York: McKay.

Gottfried, A. (1983). Research in review. Intrinsic motivation in young children. *Young Children, 39*(1), 64–73.

Greenberg, M. (1976). Research in music in early childhood education: A survey with recommendations. *Council for Research in Music Education, 45,* 1–20.

Greenspan, S., & Greenspan, N. T. (1985). *First feelings: Milestones in the emotional development of your baby and child.* New York: Viking.

Griffin, E. F. (1982). *The island of childhood: Education in the special world of nursery school.* Teachers College Press, Columbia University.

Hawkins, D. (1970). Messing about in science. *ESS Reader.* Newton, MA: Education Development Center.

Hendrick, J. (1986). *Total learning: Curriculum for the young child* (2nd ed.). Columbus, OH: Merrill.

Herron, R., & Sutton-Smith, B. (1974). *Child's play.* New York: Wiley.

Hill, D. (1979). *Mud, sand, and water.* Washington, DC: NAEYC.

Hirsch, E. (Ed.). (1984). *The block book.* Washington, DC: NAEYC.

Hoffman, M. L. (1975). Moral internalization, parental power, and the nature of parent-child interaction. *Developmental Psychology, 11,* 228–239.

Holt, B. (1979). *Science with young children.* Washington, DC: NAEYC.

Honig, A. S. (1980). The young child and you—learning together. *Young Children, 35*(4), 2–10.

Honig, A. S. (1981). What are the needs of infants? *Young Children, 37*(1), 3–10.

Honig, A. S. (1982). Parent involvement in early childhood education. In B. Spodek (Ed.), *Handbook of research in early childhood education.* New York: Free Press.

Honig, A. S. (1985). Research in review. Compliance, control, and discipline (Parts 1 & 2). *Young Children, 40*(2) 50–58; *40*(3) 47–52.

Honig, A. S. (1986). Research in review. Stress and coping in children (Parts 1 & 2). *Young Children, 41*(4) 50–63; *41*(5) 47–59.

Kamii, C. (1982). *Number in preschool and kindergarten.* Washington, DC: NAEYC.

Kamii, C. (1985). Leading primary education toward excellence: Beyond worksheets and drill. *Young Children, 40*(6), 3–9.

Kamii, C., & DeVries, R. (1980). *Group games in early education.* Washington, DC: NAEYC.

Kamii, C., & Lee-Katz, L. (1979). Physics in early childhood education: A Piagetian approach. *Young Children, 34*(4), 4–9.

Katz, L. (1980). Mothering and teaching: Some significant distinctions. In L. Katz (Ed.), *Current topics in early childhood education* (Vol. 3, pp. 47–64). Norwood, NJ: Ablex.

Kitano, M. (1982). Young gifted children: Strategies for preschool teachers. *Young Children, 37*(4), 14–24.

Kline, L. W. (1985). *Learning to read, teaching to read.* Newark, DE: LWK Enterprises.

Kobak, D. (1979). Teaching children to care. *Children Today, 8,* 6–7, 34–35.

Kohlberg, L., & Mayer, R. (1972). Development as the aim of education. *Harvard Educational Review, 42,* 449–496.

Kopp, C. B. (1982). Antecedents of self-regulation: A developmental perspective. *Developmental Psychology, 18,* 199–214.

Kuczynski, L. (1983). Reasoning, prohibitions, and motivations for compliance. *Developmental Psychology, 19,* 126–134.

Languis, M., Sanders, T., & Tipps, S. (1980). *Brain and learning: Directions in early childhood education.* Washington, DC: NAEYC.

Lasky, L., & Mukerji, R. (1980). *Art: Basic for young children.* Washington, DC: NAEYC.

Lay-Dopyera, M., & Dopyera, J. (1986). Strategies for teaching. In C. Seefeldt (Ed.), *Early childhood curriculum: A review of current research.* New York: Teachers College Press, Columbia University.

Lightfoot, S. (1978). *Worlds apart: Relationships between families and schools.* New York: Basic.

Lickona, T. (1983). *Raising good children.* New York: Bantam.

Lozoff, B., Brillenham, G., Trause, M. A., Kennell, J. H., & Klaus, M. H. (1977, July). The mother-newborn relationship: Limits of adaptability. *Journal of Pediatrics, 91.*

Lytton, H. (1979). Disciplinary encounters between young boys and their mothers and fathers: Is there a contingency system? *Developmental Psychology, 15,* 256–268.

McAfee, O. (1985). Research report. Circle time: Getting past "Two Little Pumpkins." *Young Children, 40*(6), 24–29.

McCracken, J. B. (Ed.). (1986). *Reducing stress in young children's lives.* Washington, DC: NAEYC.

McDonald, D. T. (1979). *Music in our lives: The early years.* Washington, DC: NAEYC.

Meisels, S. (1985). *Developmental screening in early childhood.* Washington, DC: NAEYC.

Miller, C. S. (1984). Building self-control: Discipline for young children. *Young Children, 40*(1), 15–19.

Montessori, M. (1964). *The Montessori method.* Cambridge, MA: Robert Bentley.

Moore, S. (1982). Prosocial behavior in the early years: Parent and peer influences. In B. Spodek (Ed.), *Handbook of research in early childhood education.* New York: Free Press.

Mussen, P., & Eisenberg-Bert, N. (1977). *Roots of caring, sharing, and helping: The development of prosocial behavior in children.* San Francisco: Freeman.

NAEYC. (1982). *Early childhood teacher education guidelines for four- and five-year programs.* Washington, DC: NAEYC.

NAEYC. (1984). *Accreditation criteria and procedures of the National Academy of Early Childhood Programs.* Washington, DC: NAEYC.

NAEYC. (1985). *Guidelines for early childhood education programs in associate degree granting institutions.* Washington, DC: NAEYC.

National Institute of Education. (1984). *Becoming a nation of readers: The report of the Commission on Reading.* Washington, DC: U.S. Department of Education.

Piaget, J. (1950). *The psychology of intelligence.* London: Routledge & Kegan Paul.

Piaget, J. (1952). *The origins of intelligence in children.* (M. Cook, Trans.). New York: Norton. (Original work published 1936)

Piaget, J. (1972). *Science of education and the psychology of the child* (rev. ed.). New York: Viking. (Original work published 1965)

Powell, D. (1986). Effects of program approaches and teaching practices. *Young Children, 41*(6), 60–67.

Ramsey, P. G. (1979). Beyond "Ten Little Indians" and turkeys: Alternative approaches to Thanksgiving. *Young Children, 34*(6), 28–32, 49–52.

Ramsey, P. G. (1982). Multicultural education in early childhood. *Young Children, 37*(2), 13–24.

Read, K. H., Gardner, P., & Mahler, B. (1986). *Early childhood programs: A laboratory for human relationships* (8th ed.). New York: Holt, Rinehart & Winston.

Riley, S. S. (1984). *How to generate values in young children: Integrity, honesty, individuality, self-confidence.* Washington, DC: NAEYC.

Rogers, D. L., & Ross, D. D. (1986). Encouraging positive social interaction among young children. *Young Children, 41*(3), 12–17.

Rubin, K., & Everett, B. (1982). Social perspective-taking in young children. In S. G. Moore & C. R. Cooper (Eds.), *The young child: Reviews of research* (Vol. 3, pp. 97–114). Washington, DC: NAEYC.

Ruopp, R., Travers, J., Glantz, F., & Coelen, C. (1979). *Children at the center. Final report of the National Day Care Study* (Vol. 1). Cambridge, MA: Abt Associates.

Sackoff, E., & Hart, R. (1984, Summer). Toys: Research and applications. *Children's Environments Quarterly,* 1–2.

Saracho, O., & Spodek, B. (Eds.). (1983). *Understanding the multicultural experience in early childhood education.* Washington, DC: NAEYC.

Schachter, F. F., & Strage, A. A. (1982). Adults' talk and children's language development. In S. G. Moore & C. R. Cooper (Eds.), *The young child: Reviews of research* (Vol. 3, pp. 79–96). Washington, DC: NAEYC.

Schaffer, H. R. (1984). *The child's entry into a social world.* Orlando, FL: Academic.

Schickedanz, J. (1986). *More than the ABCs: The early stages of reading and writing.* Washington, DC: NAEYC.

Schickedanz, J., Schickedanz, D. I., & Forsyth, P. D. (1982). *Toward understanding children.* Boston: Little, Brown.

Seefeldt, C. (1986). The visual arts. In C. Seefeldt (Ed.), *The early childhood curriculum: A review of current research.* New York: Teachers College Press, Columbia University.

Shure, M. B., & Spivack, G. (1978). *Problem-solving techniques in childrearing.* San Francisco: Jossey-Bass.

Skeen, P., Garner, A. P., & Cartwright, S. (1984). *Woodworking for young children.* Washington, DC: NAEYC.

Smith, C. A., & Davis, D. E. (1976). Teaching children non-sense. *Young Children, 34*(3), 4–11.

Smith, F. (1982). *Understanding reading.* New York: Holt, Rinehart & Winston.

Smith, F. (1985). *Reading without nonsense* (2nd ed.). New York: Teachers College Press, Columbia University.

Smith, N. (1983). *Experience and art: Teaching children to paint.* New York: Teachers College Press, Columbia University.

Souweine, J., Crimmins, S., & Mazel, C. (1981). *Mainstreaming: Ideas for teaching young children.* Washington, DC: NAEYC.

Sparling, J. (1984). *Learning games for the first three years.* New York: Walker.

Spodek, B. (1985). *Teaching in the early years* (3rd ed.). Englewood Cliffs, NJ: Prentice-Hall.

Spodek, B. (Ed.). (1986). *Today's kindergarten: Exploring its knowledge base, extending its curriculum.* New York: Teachers College Press, Columbia University.

Sponseller, D. (1982). Play and early education. In B. Spodek (Ed.), *Handbook of research in early childhood education.* New York: Free Press.

Sprung, B. (1978). *Perspectives on non-sexist early childhood education.* New York: Teachers College Press, Columbia University.

Sroufe, L. A. (1979). The coherence of individual development. *American Psychologist, 34,* 834–841.

Standards for educational and psychological testing. (1985). Washington, DC: American Psychological Association, American Educational Research Association, and National Council on Measurement in Education.

Stewart, I. S. (1982). The real world of teaching two-year-old children. *Young Children, 37*(5), 3–13.

Stone, J. G. (1978). *A guide to discipline* (rev. ed.). Washington, DC: NAEYC.

Uphoff, J.K., & Gilmore, J. (1985, September). Pupil age at school entrance—how many are ready for success? *Educational Leadership, 43,* 86–90.

Veach, D. M. (1977). Choice with responsibility. *Young Children, 32*(4), 22–25.

Wallinga, C. R., & Sweaney, A. L. (1985). A sense of *real* accomplishment: Young children as productive family members. *Young Children, 41*(1), 3–9.

Warren, R. M. (1977). *Caring: Supporting children's growth.* Washington, DC: NAEYC.

Weber, E. (1984). *Ideas influencing early childhood education: A theoretical analysis.* New York: Teachers College Press, Columbia University.

Weissbourd, B. (1981). Supporting parents as people. In B. Weissbourd & J. Musick (Eds.), *Infants: Their social environments.* Washington, DC: NAEYC.

Wellman, H. M. (1982). The foundations of knowledge: Concept development in the young child. In S. G. Moore & C. R. Cooper (Eds.), *The young child: Reviews of research* (Vol. 3, pp. 115–134). Washington, DC: NAEYC.

Willert, M., & Kamii, C. (1985). Reading in kindergarten: Direct versus indirect teaching. *Young Children, 40*(4), 3–9.

Willis, A., & Ricciuti, H. (1975). *A good beginning for babies: Guidelines for group care.* Washington, DC: NAEYC.

Wolfgang, C. H., & Glickman, C. D. (1980). *Solving discipline problems.* Boston: Allyn & Bacon.

Yarrow, M. R., Scott, P. M., & Waxler, C. Z. (1973). Learning concern for others. *Developmental Psychology, 8,* 240–260.

Yarrow, M. R., & Waxler, C. Z. (1976). Dimensions and correlates of prosocial behavior in young children. *Child Development, 47,* 118–125.

Zavitkovsky, D., Baker, K. R., Berlfein, J. R., & Almy, M. (1986). *Listen to the children.* Washington, DC: NAEYC.

Ziegler, P. (1985). Saying good-bye to preschool. *Young Children, 40*(3), 11–15.

PART 2

Developmentally Appropriate Care for Children From Birth to Age 3

During the development of NAEYC's Criteria for center accreditation through the National Academy of Early Childhood Programs, a committee from the National Center for Clinical Infant Programs (NCCIP) reviewed the document with particular attention to the way in which the Criteria addressed the care of infants and toddlers in groups. In many cases, the accreditation Criteria are written generally, with references to developmentally appropriate activities, materials, or interactions among staff and children.

This document, written by that NCCIP committee, provides more specific details about what is appropriate for infants and toddlers in group care.

Prepared by the members of the Day Care Committee of the National Center for Clinical Infant Programs
> **J. Ronald Lally**
> **Sally Provence, M.D.**
> **Eleanor Szanton**
> **Bernice Weissbourd**

Introduction

Developmentally appropriate programs for children from birth to age 3 are distinctly different from all other types of programs—they are *not* a scaled-down version of a good program for preschool children. These program differences are determined by the unique characteristics and needs of children during the first 3 years:

- changes take place far more rapidly in infancy than during any other period in life
- during infancy, as at every other age, all areas of development—cognitive, social, emotional, and physical—are intertwined
- infants are totally dependent on adults to meet their needs
- very young children are especially vulnerable to adversity because they are less able to cope actively with discomfort or stress

We will first look at how infants develop, and then consider some of the basic elements of appropriate infant care derived from this information.

How infants and toddlers develop
The early months

All infants are unique individuals whose needs and states vary from moment to moment. Adults must sensitively respond to infants' changing signals. Consistent caregiving is vital. Schedules are adjusted according to the child's eating and sleeping rhythms. Holding and touching are determined by infants' preferences for body contact, although they depend on being carried as an introduction to sensory and motor experiences. Through these responsive interactions, infants develop a sense of a benevolent, orderly world worthy of their attention.

Newborns enter the world ready for social contact. During the first 9 months they come to distinguish friends from strangers. They initiate social interactions. They make sounds and movements that communicate pleasure, surprise, anger, disappointment, anxiety, and other feelings. They develop expectations about people's behavior based on how parents and others treat them. They thrive on frequent, responsive eye contact. They delight in hearing language and other sounds. Babies may beam or calm themselves when they are held close by adults who enjoy warm physical contact.

Through these social interactions with benevolent, affectionate adults, infants begin to develop their first positive love relationships. This development of trust and emotional security comes about because babies

Through responsive interactions, infants develop a sense of a benevolent, orderly world worthy of their attention.

learn to expect positive experiences.

Therefore, if babies are to trust us, we must quickly answer their cries of distress. We must respect their individual tempo and sensitivity—if a noise startles a baby when she or he pushes a button on the activity board, we offer another less frightening activity.

This responsive communication with adults who are attuned to children helps to encourage and expand their verbal and nonverbal responses. Children begin to learn about sensory experiences, motor actions, and expressions of feelings even when they don't understand most of the words.

For very young infants, movement itself is particularly enriching. As they move their arms, legs, and other body parts, through touching and being touched, babies begin to become more aware of their body's boundaries. They soon discover they can change what they see, hear, or feel through their own activity—how delightful to shake their foot and hear the bell on the sock jingle!

Before children can creep or crawl, they depend on adults to carry them to an interesting event (such as placing them in front of a mirror) or to bring an object or activity to them. If infants are deprived of many opportunities to sample a variety of sensory and motor experiences, their emotional and cognitive development will be hampered.

A sense of well-being and emotional security conveyed by warm and responsive adults creates a learning base from which children can benefit by even more experiences. Safe in the arms of one who cares for them, they can confidently turn the handle on a jack-in-the-box, roll a ball with sparkling shapes inside it, or investigate other intriguing objects. This sense of wonder and excitement about the world can permeate a child's approach to learning far into the future.

Crawlers and walkers

Freedom to move about safely is vital for infants who are beginning to crawl or walk. While they continue to need warmth and individual attention, infants move at their own pace away from, and back to, the security of a loving adult.

Joan, 13¾ months, and Curtis, 17 months, were playing on the floor near the bookcase. They were climbing in and out of the doll bed, scrambling over each other to do so. Then Curtis got too close to Joan, wedging her in. She cried until Gina picked her up and gave her a hug. Her good humor restored, Joan climbed on the yellow truck and half sat, half leaned on it. She inspected it as she ate a cracker, then meandered about the room and climbed into the large rocking chair, where she sat rocking again.

She approached Jerry once, and as Jerry talked to her she patted Jerry's notebook, then toddled off to crawl under the crib where she sat peering out between the bars of the lowered cribside for a minute or two. Next, she crawled out without bumping her head, stood, and toddled around the room again, looking closely at what Leslie, Curtis, and Jackie were doing, but not involving herself in any of it.

*****

Once, when Martha picked up Jackie, Joan crawled across the floor, pulled to a stand at her knee, and seemed to be letting Martha know that she didn't want her to hold Jackie. Martha reached down, patted her head, and said, "What's the matter, Joan, don't you have anything to do?" Joan seemed to be satisfied with this attention and again became involved in her investigation of available toys. She frequently returned to Martha for brief contacts, receiving a smile, a pat, or a word, after which she would resume her activity in the room.

Interpretation: Gina and Martha allowed Joan plenty of time to explore what *she* wanted to—the truck, the rocking chair, the notebook, the world from behind crib bars, and three other children. Only twice did the adults directly interact with her, but they were strategic moments: Once when she was physically uncomfortable and once when she approached. Gina responded not only by removing Joan from the source of discomfort, but also by physically reminding her she was loved. Martha, too, turned some of Joan's approaches into brief verbal exchanges, which apparently satisfied her when she seemed to need more frequent refueling.

* * *

Children's awareness of their emotions and abilities expands when a responsive adult identifies and elaborates on their feelings and perceptions, even before they talk. An adult might say, for example, "You're wondering what will happen if you try to fit that cup in the box. Will it be too big? Too little? Or j-u-s-t right?" As infants become more mobile and verbal, their secure base can be reached as much through eyes and ears as by physical contact.

In a benevolent and safe environment, mobile infants thrive when they are expected to be competent and exhibit appropriate social behaviors.

Competencies. Infants can become deeply engrossed in perfecting their many skills. In high-quality programs for infants at this stage, the children are offered choices from a wide variety of materials to play with and to explore. When children direct their own play, they see themselves as competent people—a major building block in feeling good about themselves.

Daily routines such as baths and diapering can also continue to be creative times to enhance physical growth, cognitive skills, and communication.

When provided with a wealth of experiences to choose from during the day, infants seek desired activities or objects and learn to avoid painful or fearful situations. They also begin to understand, in a practical sensorimotor way, such concepts as cause and effect; the use of tools; and familiarity with distance, spatial relationships, and perspectives. They begin to group and compare. They imitate. They develop patterns of relating to others, including adults. They express themselves vocally with increasing specificity. Therefore, they need to be encouraged to explore and learn from a rich array of activities, objects, and people.

Terry (10 months) was playing with an aluminum margarine cup and an ice cream stick. He hit the cup with the stick several times and caused it to flip over. He then used the stick to scoot the upside-down cup along the floor. For 10 minutes, he continued with great concentration, as he alternately flipped and pushed the cup and observed what happened.

Later, while in the kitchen with Kathy, who was preparing food, he discovered the dishwasher and found he could roll the lower rack in and out. He kept pushing it in and pulling it out, smiling with pleasure as he listened to the changing clatter of the dishes. He then poked about in the soap well for several minutes. All of this was done in an engrossed, exploratory manner. Kathy spoke to him occasionally and commented on what he was doing, but allowed him to carry through his project in his own way.

Ellen Levine Ebert

The development of trust and emotional security comes about because babies learn to expect positive experiences. Therefore, if babies are to trust us, we must quickly answer their cries of distress.

Interpretation: In this situation, Terry *was* playing with a rich array of physical stimuli, none of which were expensive toys. An empty margarine cup, an ice cream stick, and a piece of kitchen equipment were all he needed. Kathy wisely allowed him the chance to roll the rack, ready to intervene only if that activity threatened the dishes. By commenting on his activities, she enabled him to absorb what language he could—long before he was able to use language himself—to begin to put together an experience and the words that describe it.

*   *   *

Still later during this period, mobile infants begin to use and manipulate tools (such as dipping water with a cup), to see objects as three-dimensional (for example, climbing inside a box), and to prolong or change sounds or action (such as pulling a train back and forth with the bell clanging).

These new-found skills arise as children creep, crawl, cruise, walk, climb, and descend stairs safely. Infants develop small muscle skills when they grasp, drop, pull, push, throw, nest, finger, and mouth objects. They develop their first words, usually the names of important adults or objects, and action words. Because there are so many things to stimulate infants, sensitive adults will ensure that a good balance is maintained in the levels of intensity of play, from active . . . to quiet . . . to sleep.

Social behaviors. Mobile infants are naturally very curious about other children. Friendships begin to emerge. Because infants are not yet experienced in interacting with each other, however, they often require assistance in doing so.

Leslie had become rather adept at getting what she wanted and avoiding what she didn't. Sitting on the floor with Terry one day, she watched him playing with an hourglass full of colorful beads. She looked intently, then reached over and took it from him. Terry, who did not protest, was handed an identical toy by Jerry. Leslie again observed Terry, dropped her own hourglass, and again took his. She did this with four identical toys, always wanting the one Terry had. Finally, he protested and squealed but was unable to retain the toy against her pull. When Terry cried, Jerry, with a comment, stepped in and returned Terry's property. He separated them a little and saw that each child had a toy.

*****

Leslie and Terry, age 5 months, were sitting in the playpen with several toys. They were intently engaged with the toys while the adults were busy with other children. Leslie seemed oblivious of Terry's presence as she vigorously and repeatedly banged a rubber giraffe on the floor, apparently fascinated by the squeak her activity produced. When her attention was diverted by Terry's moving foot, she stared at it intently, grasped it, and

tried unsuccessfully to bring it to her mouth. With a quizzical expression, she repeatedly stared at, grasped, and released it. She was distracted briefly by the sound of the music box, then went back to Terry's foot. She seemed to become frustrated at not being able to pick it up and put it into her mouth, and started to make complaining sounds, which soon became angry crying. She was picked up and comforted by Martha, who asked her what the trouble was, and explained in a comforting voice that it was Terry's foot, not a toy, she was reaching for.

Interpretation: It is often very hard for an adult to know exactly when to intervene between children. In the first case, the caregiver monitored but *did not* intervene until Terry protested, and he neither punished nor reprimanded Leslie. Although Leslie took Terry's toys, she was probably not competing with him, nor did she necessarily want all of the toys for herself. It seems more likely that the toy Terry had was animated by his movement of it and thus more attractive than

A sense of well-being and emotional security conveyed by warm and responsive adults creates a learning base from which children can benefit by even more experiences.

In a benevolent and safe environment, mobile infants thrive when they are expected to be competent and exhibit appropriate social behaviors.

her own toy. It was as though at this stage she was not aware of the sameness of the toys and did not realize that she could create the same movement with her own. Terry's failure to protest for a time permitted her to continue. While one does not imagine that at this age she learned anything definite about the rights of others, in this exchange she did have to adapt to the adult's intervention.

In the second case, the caregiver intervened only when Leslie became frustrated. She then responded by not only physically breaking up the frustrating situation, but also by stating why Leslie was frustrated. Even though this explanation was undoubtedly beyond Leslie's capacity to understand, she could respond to the comforting and the tone of voice which ideally contained at one and the same time sympathy and a "this is how the world works" character.

* * *

Children's relationships can at one minute seem very sophisticated as they imitate a gentle, patient, or generous adult. At other times, fatigue, anxiety, or other distress overwhelms such young children. Adults must expect this great variability in social interaction and be prepared to guide children toward their own solutions.

One typical problem that arises when infants become mobile is the intense possessiveness that emerges when one child wants another's toy (or snack, or time with a special person). Forcing children to share, contrary to folk wisdom, is not an effective way to help children learn to share. An ample number of

toys must be provided. More importantly, children are more likely to share when generous adults share with them.

Children also must experience many attempts to negotiate ownership, so they can develop a sense of another child's perspective as well. They need to gain confidence that a shared item will be returned to them, because they are still learning that objects exist even when they are not in sight. Only in this type of accepting atmosphere will infants begin to understand the value of and reciprocity involved in the social skill called *sharing*. In a good program, adults respect children's choice to share only when the children are willing to do so.

Toddlers and 2-year-olds

Competencies. Toddlers and 2-year-olds thrive on exploration and creativity. They enjoy fantasy (such as pretending a toy dog is alive or using a piece of cloth as a blanket), when props are selected to encourage productive play. When their needs have been met appropriately as infants, toddlers are experienced in making choices and implementing their own ideas.

Toddlers' imagination and curiosity give them great energy and creative potential. They need opportunities to develop and express these capacities. Toddlers rely on adults to help them deal with their intense feelings and rapid fluctuations in moods. Adults must be especially careful to give toddlers many chances to figure

21

things out for themselves, while remaining available to them if they ask for assistance.

Toddlers begin to divide objects into categories. For example, they might line up all the large rubber animals for a parade and leave the small ones in the zoo. Unstructured materials for art, music, dance, and dramatic play enable children to enjoy the process of creating their own ideas and solving their own problems.

Toddlers are entering a new phase of mental activity. In addition to growing familiarity with symbols, they speak with increasing sophistication. Out of these early, relatively abstract ideas will come an understanding of adult words, numbers, and linguistic and scientific symbols. Toddlers need experiences in the use of common language and shared meaning.

The thinking of toddlers is very different from that of older children or adults. For example, they believe that all moving things are alive. The period from 18 to 36 months is filled with exploration, questioning, discovery, and a continual determination to find meaning in events, objects, and ideas.

Gina brought a small scooter into the room and Jackie (11 months) took it immediately. He pushed it as he crawled behind it, turned it over, examined it carefully, and pulled to a stand on it and pushed it as he walked behind. Even when it tipped over, causing him to fall, he was undaunted and continued his pursuit. For 10 or 15 minutes he pushed, pulled, tipped over, and uprighted the scooter before discovering how to climb on it. Then, seated on it, he soon discovered how to push it backward. He was delighted with his newfound toy and Gina responded to his pleasure with animation and encouraging comments. He smiled and gurgled, making almost continuous "ooh" sounds in a soft, happy voice.

Interpretation: The importance of the presence of an intelligent, benevolent, and affectionate adult in facilitating infants' development cannot be overemphasized. Developmental progress occurs through a process of interaction between children and their environment, especially with the adults who care for them. Experiences in which they acquire a new skill or master some developmental task are a part of development. The adult should be able to judge children's abilities and decide how to help and support them.

Gina encouraged, supported, and appreciated Jackie's many activities with the scooter. Jackie must have experienced pleasure in learning while observing the different things that happened to the scooter in relation to his manipulation of it. Freedom to use his initiative and curiosity was important; interference from another might have robbed him of the experience of examination, evaluation, trial, and mastery in this situation. Gina protected him from intrusion and encour-

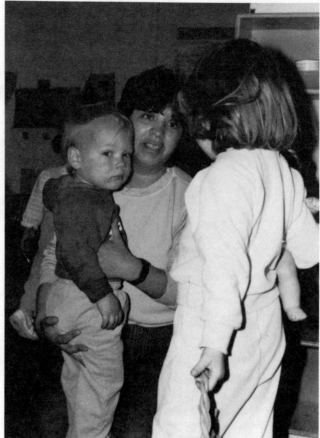

Children's relationships can at one minute seem very sophisticated as they imitate a gentle, patient, or generous adult. At other times, fatigue, anxiety, or other distress overwhelms such young children.

Subjects & Predicates

aged him. There was no doubt about his pleasure in what he was doing or that he had learned something. An astronomer discovering a planet could not have been more eloquent in communicating the excitement and joy of discovery.

* * *

Once we understand that toddlers learn by active involvement with people and by manipulating objects, it becomes clear that such activities as coloring books, worksheets, and models made of clay or other materials that children are expected to imitate are inappropriate.

Toilet learning frequently becomes the paramount issue during the third year of life. Parents and staff should agree upon an approach for helping children learn this new aspect of self-control. Professionals must ensure that common, but inappropriate, techniques such as punishment or shaming children are not used in the child care setting. Toilet learning can only be effective if the child wants to learn, and feels responsible. It must be accomplished in a spirit of cooperation and enthusiasm as children reach this milestone in their development.

With David, the course of toilet learning was not entirely smooth, though not really difficult. The staff began suggesting that he might like to go to the potty when he was 19 months and started removing his diaper and putting him on the potty chair. The first day he usually wet himself as his diaper was being removed. However, on the second day he had a bowel movement on the pot and seemed very pleased with himself. For the next few days he would occasionally urinate or defecate in the pot with some pleasure.

Then he entered a period when he wasn't sure the whole thing was a good idea at all. At 20½ months, when asked to go to the pot, he answered vehemently, "No pot, no pot!" He was taken anyway but did nothing, though a few minutes after he was off the potty and back in his training pants, he wet himself.

Then for a time David's attendance was irregular, making it more difficult for him and the staff to pursue his toilet learning in the center. At 26 months, he adamantly refused the pot and efforts were simply suspended for a time. A note was made that he did not mind being wet and did not indicate any wish to be changed when wet. However, he was not protesting the change of diapers and was very lively and happy, interacting in a playful way with Kathy, his major caregiver.

When he was 26½ months, an observation which suggested that his oppositional behavior had something specific to do with Kathy as well as with his mother was made. While he would not go to the potty for Kathy, he would allow any one of three other staff members to take him and seemed very happy and pleased with himself at such times. This is a good example of a typical kind of struggle often seen around toilet learning: The child wishes both to learn and not to learn to use the toilet, and may express one side of his feelings with one person and the other side with others. Responding to this cue from David, we arranged that for a time he be taken to the potty by someone other than Kathy. He then began to ask to be taken and to be pleased with his own mastery. At 27 months, he was using the toilet willingly, standing to urinate, and was wearing a diaper only at naptime. A week later, the note was made that the only time he wet himself was while napping, but he rejected any attempt to put a diaper on during his nap. By the time another week had passed, he either took himself to the bathroom or asked to be taken, having gained full control and having assumed responsibility for self-regulation in this area.

*****

Larry, 25 months, was sitting in the wooden carriage next to the sandbox. He began to look very sad and started crying. When Martha asked what was wrong, he didn't answer. When she picked him up she discovered he was wet. He had been asked several times during the morning whether he wanted to go to the potty and had

Once we understand that toddlers learn by active involvement with people and by manipulating objects, it becomes clear that such activities as coloring books, worksheets, and models made of clay or other materials that children are expected to imitate are inappropriate.

Young children come to value themselves if they have been valued.

refused each time. She took him to be changed and he cried the entire time, until she reminded him that she was not going to spank him. With that reassurance, he stopped crying while she finished dressing him, and went back to play until lunchtime.

Interpretation: In both of these situations, the caregivers followed the cues of the child and the family, continually encouraging toilet learning through reminders, actual trips to the potty, and praise, but without punishment or shaming when expectations were not met.

* * *

Social behaviors. The social awareness of toddlers and 2-year-olds is vastly more complex than that of younger infants. Their past experiences in communicating with others enable them to refine their ability to read children's and adults' signals. Their feelings of empathy bloom as they continue to see that other people have feelings too. They increasingly imitate others.

One of the most important sources of toddlers' self-esteem is the continuity of relationships with loving adults. Young children come to value themselves if they have been valued. This esteem in turn makes them receptive to positive guidance. If adults have realistic expectations, and communicate them clearly and consistently, toddlers and 2-year-olds learn and accept the limits of appropriate and inappropriate behavior.

While they rely on adult protection and guidance, toddlers assert their awareness of their separateness from others. They feel independent and competent, and yet they realize they will depend on adults. A healthy toddler's inner world is filled with conflicting feelings—independence and dependence, pride and shame, confidence and doubt, self-awareness and confusion, fear and omnipotence, hostility and intense love, anger and tenderness, initiative and passivity. These feelings challenge parents' and staff resourcefulness and knowledge to provide emotional security.

For this age group, sound emotional development is derived from experiences that support initiative, cre-

24

ativity, autonomy, and self-esteem and yet recognize that the children are still very young. Toddlers strive to be independent and self-reliant, and yet they need to count on affection and comfort.

Toddlers and 2-year-olds need opportunities to be responsible, to make significant choices, and to be challenged or disciplined in ways that keep their dignity intact. They are beginning to understand why certain behavior must be limited—that rules are fair and judgments just. They need to feel these limits are placed on them by adults who can be counted on and who mean what they say. These are adults who can support them in their frustrations and disappointments and enjoy their pleasures and successes with them.

They need guidance in how to express their often intense and hostile feelings in acceptable ways. If toddlers and 2-year-olds do not have the guidance of adults who understand and plan appropriately for them, they may experience severe stress and conflict. A group of young children without adequate adult support can become a chaotic environment in which child development is severely impaired. The next section will examine the details of the basic elements in appropriate infant care.

Basic elements of appropriate care for infants and toddlers

Particularly in the preverbal and early verbal years, observations of child behavior, and of child-adult and child-child interaction, provide essential information about children and their caregivers. Assessments about the extent to which the adult, whether parent or other caregiver, is in tune with a child and whether a child is progressing in a healthy manner are derived in large measure from observation augmented by insights and information provided by the adults who know the child best—usually parents.

General knowledge about infants and young children from theoretical, philosophical, and practical sources provides a necessary conceptual framework. Within that framework, however, one must have the benefit of seeing and knowing the individual child in order to plan, provide, and evaluate those experiences that will facilitate healthy development.

For the first few months of life, warm, supportive, and dependable adult-child contact is essential if infants are to develop a sense of security and trust. As infants begin to crawl, they use these early feelings of confidence and competence to explore new environments. They also must have the opportunity to return safely to the base of a readily available, loving caregiver.

Then as older toddlers and 2-year-olds, children who are secure and trusting will be increasingly ready to take initiative, be creative, participate in a group, and assert themselves as individuals. An atmosphere of affectionate attention is essential for healthy development throughout childhood.

What kinds of interactions and activities are characteristic of this type of atmosphere?

Patient, warm adults

Patient, warm adults are probably the most important factor in a developmentally appropriate program for infants and toddlers. From birth, children take an active role in their interaction with others. Adults who work well with children younger than age 3 are aware of the need to mesh their behaviors with each child's unique style of approaching people and objects.

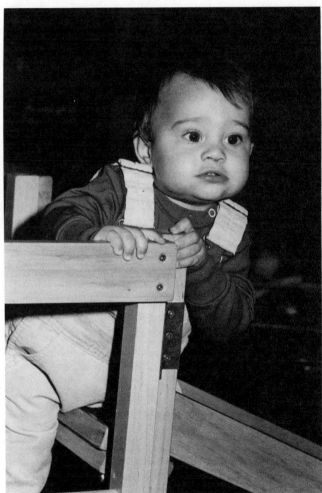

Tyroler & Cooper

Toddlers and 2-year-olds need opportunities to be responsible, to make significant choices, and to be challenged or disciplined in ways that keep their dignity intact.

Routines are the curriculum. The following examples illustrate how important it is to make the most of every minute of a young child's day.

When put in his highchair for lunch, Jackie (10 months) was quiet. He remained so while Joan (13 months), who was hungry and irritable, was put in her chair. As soon as he saw her plate of food, however, Jackie began to fuss and kick impatiently. Gina put some bits of corned beef hash and green beans on his tray, and he quieted for about 5 minutes as he picked up small pieces with his thumb and index finger, and ate them.

Once in a while, he stopped eating to look at Joan. He listened as Gina talked with Joan about what she was eating and about how well Joan was using her spoon. As Gina began to feed Jackie, he reached toward her mouth with a bean, then smiled with pleasure when she ate it and said, "Oh, that's good Jackie. Thank you." A bit later, while he was fed pudding, he insisted on holding the spoon so Gina took another.

Joan, by now, was beginning to smear her food on her highchair tray. Gina did not interfere. With help from Gina, Jackie held a small glass of milk and took a sip or two, but managed to spill much of it. He slid down in his chair, rubbed his eyes, appeared sleepy, and pulled at his bib. Gina took him out of the chair and held him on her lap as she helped Joan finish her meal. Joan then played on the floor as Gina washed Jackie's hands and face and got him ready for his nap.

Interpretation: Gina knew from her observations that Jackie was able to pick up small bits of food and feed himself, and she set things up to allow him to do so. Joan, just 3 months older, had more capacity for self-feeding than Jackie. Gina's ability to keep contact with both children was noteworthy. She was there to give help to each child as needed, to encourage self-feeding, and to keep the meal pleasant. It is very hard for most young children, even after they are capable of self-feeding, to do so without adult support.

The art of being available to help children eat while also allowing them to work at self-feeding is not easy for some adults. There is a tendency to either do it all for the child or to expect the child to do it alone. Time, patience, and the capacity to be pleased with gradual change are required. The adult must also be able to accept some messiness as the child handles and smears the food.

* * *

Even newborns sense whether someone enjoys their company during play and everyday routines such as diapering.

Martha was bathing Leslie (4 months), who was happy, smiling, and relaxed as Martha talked with her. Leslie reached for a container of shampoo nearby. Martha moved it out of reach and put a small, red plastic fish into the water to attract Leslie's attention. She looked at it intently, moved her arms, and tried to reach and grasp it, splashing the water. This activity seemed to fascinate her and she continued to splash more and more actively, squealing with delight. A little later, she watched intently as Martha squeezed water out of the sponge. Before her bath was finished she succeeded, after several attempts, in grasping the floating fish with both hands.

*****

Jackie (8½ months) was sitting quietly in a large, deep sink playing with a plastic shampoo bottle while Gina washed his hair. He soon reached for the soap dish and the plastic cup on the counter until he managed to get both of them into the water. He enjoyed manipulating them as they floated about. Twice he pulled to a stand by holding the edge of the sink, smiling broadly. At one point, smiling, he held the cup out toward the observer as to show it to her. When Joan (11 months) approached the sink and put her hand on the counter, Jackie touched her hand, smiled, and gurgled at her.

Gina lifted Jackie from the water and placed him on the counter to be dried. He seemed to enjoy being rubbed with the towel. He smiled at Gina, and made happy squeals and a "da da" sound. He remained inactive, lying on his back while his diaper and shirt were put on. Gina talked with him frequently while she bathed and dressed him and Jackie responded by making soft, pleasant sounds. When placed in a sitting position to have the rest of his clothes put on, he did not try to move away, nor did he actively enter the dressing process. When he was dressed, Gina helped him stand up and invited him to look at himself in the mirror. He smiled, babbled, and waved his hand at the observer, whose reflection he could also see. He then looked at his own reflection, smiled broadly, and bounced up and down as though charmed with what he saw.

Interpretation: With infants and toddlers, giving baths, changing diapers, and dressing are frequent experiences during the day. Being bathed or dressed is as much a part of the curriculum for the infant as working a puzzle, looking at a book, building a house, or counting is for an older child. When viewed from this perspective, adults can think about how these experiences can promote an infant's development.

Infants care little about being clean or sweet-smelling, but they do relish and learn from the social contact and from varied sensations as they experience changes in temperature, texture, position, sight, sound, and smell. Because baths call for close adult attention, they are a marvelous opportunity to talk to infants about themselves, what is going on, what the infants are doing, and how they are feeling. A person who enjoys infants can easily see how the bath experience can be used to stimulate learning in a perfectly natural and informal manner.

The caregivers in each of these situations use the bathing and drying process as a time to allow the child to experiment with the behavior of objects in the water and with the properties of water. Leslie practiced how to successfully grasp a floating object—a great accom-

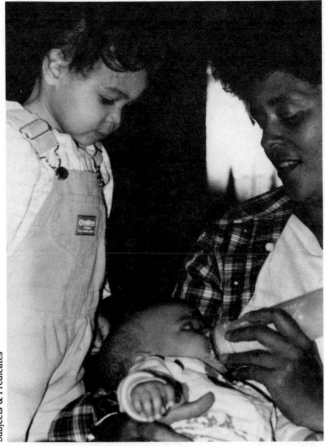

Patient, warm adults are probably the most important factor in a developmentally appropriate program for infants and toddlers.

plishment. Jackie practiced how to move his body in water. Gina used the drying process to express warmth, both physically and verbally. When Jackie saw his own body in the mirror, he was putting together what he felt with what he saw. In both cases, the infant engaged in sensorimotor learning and mastery play in association with enjoying positive social interaction with the adult.

Relating to others. Infants pick up on body language long before they can communicate verbally. Age-appropriate behaviors such as crying, messiness, dependency, willfulness, aggression, and curiosity about genital differences may make some adults uncomfortable. However, when we know these characteristics are typical, we can support infant development rather than deal with these behaviors through anger or punishment.

Curtis, 15 months, was in the playroom with Shaun, Jackie, and Joan. He silently pushed the block cart first into Jackie and then into Joan. Although an adult tried to direct him to push in another direction, he persisted in bumping into the children. He then abandoned the cart, toddled to Jackie, and pushed him over. Jackie protested by whining. Curtis moved on to Joan and tried to push her over also, but she squealed loudly and grabbed his overalls, almost pulling him down.

A few minutes later, he was sitting on the floor when Joan approached him. He reached out, grasped the seat of her pants, and pulled her down, all the time ignoring the observant adult's admonitions not to do so because it would hurt. The children were separated and he was given a jack-in-the-box, which he explored deliberately. He then spent about 2 minutes toddling about holding a squeaky toy. When he made it squeak, he smiled and looked at Karen. She smiled and commented on his making the toy squeak.

Several other times during the next hour he approached and pushed, bumped, or took toys away from smaller children. He hit at Shaun and pulled his hair. Later, he began to cry woefully. Karen went to him and he quieted briefly, then crawled a few feet away from her, lay on the floor, and broke into loud, sorrowful wails. As she soothingly talked to him, rocked him, and patted his cheek, he stopped crying and rested his head on her arm, still sobbing occasionally. He cried while she put his coat on, but once outside he was quiet while she pushed him in a cart. He was relaxed and solemn with a sorrowful expression on his face.

Interpretation: Only at the end of the morning did the several adults who had intervened to protect the other children from Curtis fully realize how many times aggressive contact was made. This situation might occur with any child of this age on any day. The adults realized that Curtis had been having difficulty adjusting to the program, so his caregiver tried to provide him with support and comfort and to help him play.

Curtis's behavior illustrates the typical difficulties young children have coping with stress. While the caregivers did not know what was going on in Curtis's mind, he was clearly unhappy much of the day and needed comfort and reassurance from his special caregiver. A young child who is unhappy and agitated, and who feels dissatisfied with adults, may be more aggressive toward other children. While Curtis's aggressive behavior had to be controlled, he needed consolation and help, not punishment.

* * *

Only by seeing that the continuity and consistency of our affectionate care is essential for children's development can we make informed decisions about the type of program we offer. Through their experiences with adults and other children, infants start the lifelong process of learning about themselves and how to get along with others. Their first feelings of empathy and mutual respect emerge when they are a part of sensitive and timely verbal and nonverbal communication.

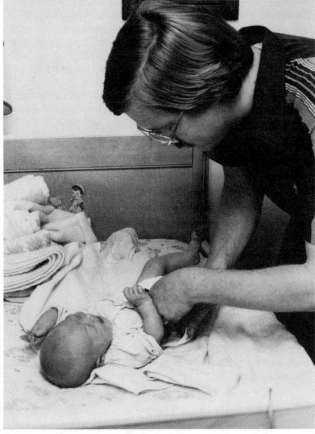

Even newborns sense whether someone enjoys their company during play and everyday routines.

Because some of the most basic elements of ethnic identity are established before age 3, infants and toddlers thrive in a setting that is culturally salient. Caregivers must recognize and support what is unique, and possibly culturally inspired, about each child. Children benefit greatly when parents and caregivers frequently and respectfully consult with each other.

Very young children also need opportunities to learn from other parts of the world around them—through a variety of colors, odors, sounds, materials, and tastes. Much of the time they play alone or in the company of a few other children. Adults who understand how children learn recognize that children gain from every experience as they initiate activities, explore new situations, engage in messy activities such as water play, use art materials, and respond to music and words.

Growth simply cannot be divided into social, emotional, physical, and cognitive development during these early years. Each child's development is individual, characterized by her or his own particular leaps, plateaus, and regressions.

Responsiveness to physical needs

Very young children cannot survive if we do not provide shelter, food, and other essential comforts. *How* these elements of survival are provided strongly affects how children see themselves and their value as people. Children come to expect an orderly world and feel motivated to develop self-control if they sense that adults respond to these physical needs as quickly as possible and with affection.

Accidents are the greatest cause of death for infants who are mobile. For this reason, their curiosity must be safely channeled without being smothered and their environment tailored to ensure their safety. All the indoor and outdoor areas, the equipment, toys, and furniture in a good program are designed to ensure children's safety, while promoting their urge to explore. Activities are monitored by a nearby adult, too.

Children can gradually be helped to learn what is safe, what is dangerous, and why. Children in a rocking boat, for example, can learn to stop rocking if another child comes near, so their fingers or feet don't get hurt. Once again, children sense they are important when they feel safe and know they will be comforted if they are injured. They also come to realize that others are similarly important.

Programs that support families

Mutual support and good communication are essential between parents and program staff. During these earliest years, children learn whether their environment is supportive, ordered, and predictable. Parents and staff who share information frequently about children's routines, unique behaviors, and daily events contribute to this sense of support.

If parents or caregivers compete with or resent each other, infants will feel the tension. Most parents have some guilt and anxiety about leaving their children in the care of another person. However, by showing support for parents as the prime adults in their children's lives, these tensions can be greatly diminished. By developing a partnership, adults see the child from a shared perspective. It is especially important that parents and caregivers discuss basic values and childrearing practices. Without such communication, children may become bewildered, confused, and anxious if there are major discrepancies between what happens at home and in the caregiving environment.

When adults share details about a child, everyone has a greater sense of the child's emerging individuality. Knowing how long a child slept or how much formula was consumed or what the child enjoyed playing with, for example, is valuable information in planning the day or evening.

As infants reach the middle of their first year, it is natural for them to become anxious around strangers, such as when their parents leave them with an unfamiliar caregiver. Stranger anxiety is a sign that children are maturing emotionally, cognitively, and socially. In a good program, parents and staff anticipate this stage and find ways to ease the difficult period, perhaps by engaging the child with an interesting toy rather than by establishing direct physical contact.

In the months that follow, as children begin to crawl and then to walk, they are better able to explore and indicate their preferences. Their favorite toys, foods, and activities can be sources of pride and interest for parents and staff alike. Infants flourish when they see their new skills appreciated by people who are important to them.

At this stage of development, the limits on their activities should be reasonably consistent between home and program. These limits, whenever possible, should be reached by mutual agreement. Parents and staff will want to talk about what activities can be encouraged at home, or how favorite foods from home might be introduced in the program.

Toddlers, too, need stable environments and understanding adults in their struggle for independence while they cling to babyhood. They work to control their emotions, which shift quickly from one extreme to another. They strive to master emerging skills that

Good programs for children from birth to age 3 are distinctly different from all other types of programs—they are *not* a scaled-down version of a good program for preschool children.

are both pleasantly exciting and anxiety-producing. Toddlers often develop their own rituals and routines to help themselves feel organized and secure.

Parents and caregivers who share knowledge about toddlers respect these developmental patterns. They should frequently discuss major events such as emotional outbursts, triumphs, and creative endeavors. In doing so, both the home and the child care program can agree on ways to provide a dependable environment that supports toddlers as they define themselves. Joint planning for toilet learning is certainly one of the most important areas that parents and teachers can collaborate on later in toddlerhood.

Summary

Infants and toddlers learn through their own experience, trial and error, repetition, imitation, and identification. Adults guide and encourage this learning by ensuring that the environment is safe and emotionally supportive. An appropriate program for children younger than age 3 invites play, active exploration, and movement. It provides a broad array of stimulating experiences within a reliable framework of routines and protection from excessive stress. Relationships with people are emphasized as an essential contribution to the quality of children's experiences.

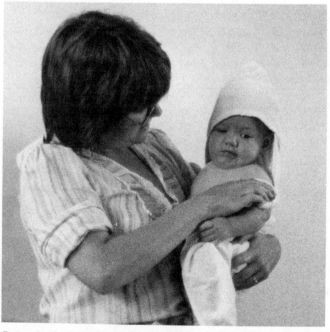

M. K. Gallagher

Being bathed or dressed is as much a part of the curriculum for the infant as working a puzzle, looking at a book, building a house, or counting is for an older child.

	Interest in others	Self-awareness	Motor milestones and eye-hand skills
The Early Months (birth through 8 months)	Newborns prefer the human face and human sound. Within the first 2 weeks, they recognize and prefer the sight, smell, and sound of the principal caregiver. Social smile and mutual gazing is evidence of early social interaction. The infant can initiate and terminate these interactions. Anticipates being lifted or fed and moves body to participate. Sees adults as objects of interest and novelty. Seeks out adults for play. Stretches arms to be taken.	Sucks fingers or hand fortuitously. Observes own hands. Places hand up as an object comes close to the face as if to protect self. Looks to the place on body where being touched. Reaches for and grasps toys. Clasps hands together and fingers them. Tries to cause things to happen. Begins to distinguish friends from strangers. Shows preference for being held by familiar people.	The young infant uses many complex reflexes: searches for something to suck; holds on when falling; turns head to avoid obstruction of breathing; avoids brightness, strong smells, and pain. Puts hand or object in mouth. Begins reaching toward interesting objects. Grasps, releases, regrasps, and releases object again. Lifts head. Holds head up. Sits up without support. Rolls over. Transfers and manipulates objects with hands. Crawls.
Crawlers and Walkers (8 to 18 months)	Exhibits anxious behavior around unfamiliar adults. Enjoys exploring objects with another as the basis for establishing relationships. Gets others to do things for child's pleasure (wind up toys, read books, get dolls). Shows considerable interest in peers. Demonstrates intense attention to adult language.	Knows own name. Smiles or plays with self in mirror. Uses large and small muscles to explore confidently when a sense of security is offered by presence of caregiver. Frequently checks for caregiver's presence. Has heightened awareness of opportunities to make things happen, yet limited awareness of responsibility for own actions. Indicates strong sense of self through assertiveness. Directs actions of others (e.g., "Sit there!"). Identifies one or more body parts. Begins to use *me, you, I.*	Sits well in chairs. Pulls self up, stands holding furniture. Walks when led. Walks alone. Throws objects. Climbs stairs. Uses marker on paper. Stoops, trots, can walk backward a few steps.
Toddlers and 2-Year-Olds (18 months to 3 years)	Shows increased awareness of being seen and evaluated by others. Sees others as a barrier to immediate gratification. Begins to realize others have rights and privileges. Gains greater enjoyment from peer play and joint exploration. Begins to see benefits of cooperation. Identifies self with children of same age or sex. Is more aware of the feelings of others. Exhibits more impulse control and self-regulation in relation to others. Enjoys small group activities.	Shows strong sense of self as an individual, as evidenced by "NO" to adult requests. Experiences self as a powerful, potent, creative doer. Explores everything. Becomes capable of self-evaluation and has beginning notions of self (good, bad, attractive, ugly). Makes attempts at self-regulation. Uses names of self and others. Identifies 6 or more body parts.	Scribbles with marker or crayon. Walks up and down stairs. Can jump off one step. Kicks a ball. Stands on one foot. Threads beads. Draws a circle. Stands and walks on tiptoes. Walks up stairs one foot on each step. Handles scissors. Imitates a horizontal crayon stroke.

Note: *This list is not intended to be exhaustive. Many of the behaviors indicated here will happen earlier or later for individual infants. The chart suggests an approximate time when a behavior might appear, but it should not be rigidly interpreted.*

Often, but not always, the behaviors appear in the order in which they emerge. Particularly for younger infants, the behaviors listed in one domain overlap considerably with several other developmental domains. Some behaviors are placed under more than one category to emphasize this interrelationship.

CHILDREN FROM BIRTH TO AGE 3

Language development/ communication	Physical, spatial, and temporal awareness	Purposeful action and use of tools	Expression of feelings
Cries to signal pain or distress. Smiles or vocalizes to initiate social contact. Responds to human voices. Gazes at faces. Uses vocal and nonvocal communication to express interest and exert influence. Babbles using all types of sounds. Engages in private conversations when alone. Combines babbles. Understands names of familiar people and objects. Laughs. Listens to conversations.	Comforts self by sucking thumb or finding pacifier. Follows a slowly moving object with eyes. Reaches and grasps toys. Looks for dropped toy. Identifies objects from various viewpoints. Finds a toy hidden under a blanket when placed there while watching.	Observes own hands. Grasps rattle when hand and rattle are both in view. Hits or kicks an object to make a pleasing sight or sound continue. Tries to resume a knee ride by bouncing to get adult started again.	Expresses discomfort and comfort/ pleasure unambiguously. Responds with more animation and pleasure to primary caregiver than to others. Can usually be comforted by familiar adult when distressed. Smiles and activates the obvious pleasure in response to social stimulation. Very interested in people. Shows displeasure at loss of social contact. Laughs aloud (belly laugh). Shows displeasure or disappointment at loss of toy. Expresses several clearly differentiated emotions: pleasure, anger, anxiety or fear, sadness, joy, excitement, disappointment, exuberance. Reacts to strangers with soberness or anxiety.
Understands many more words than can say. Looks toward 20 or more objects when named. Creates long babbled sentences. Shakes head no. Says 2 or 3 clear words. Looks at picture books with interest, points to objects. Uses vocal signals other than crying to gain assistance. Begins to use *me, you, I.*	Tries to build with blocks. If toy is hidden under 1 of 3 cloths while child watches, looks under the right cloth for the toy. Persists in a search for a desired toy even when toy is hidden under distracting objects such as pillows. When chasing a ball that rolled under sofa and out the other side, will make a detour around sofa to get ball. Pushes foot into shoe, arm into sleeve.	When a toy winds down, continues the activity manually. Uses a stick as a tool to obtain a toy. When a music box winds down, searches for the key to wind it up again. Brings a stool to use for reaching for something. Pushes away someone or something not wanted. Feeds self finger food (bits of fruit, crackers). Creeps or walks to get something or avoid unpleasantness. Pushes foot into shoe, arm into sleeve. Partially feeds self with fingers or spoon. Handles cup well with minimal spilling. Handles spoon well for self-feeding.	Actively shows affection for familiar person: hugs, smiles at, runs toward, leans against, and so forth. Shows anxiety at separation from primary caregiver. Shows anger focused on people or objects. Expresses negative feelings. Shows pride and pleasure in new accomplishments. Shows intense feelings for parents. Continues to show pleasure in mastery. Asserts self, indicating strong sense of self.
Combines words. Listens to stories for a short while. Speaking vocabulary may reach 200 words. Develops fantasy in language. Begins to play pretend games. Defines use of many household items. Uses compound sentences. Uses adjectives and adverbs. Recounts events of the day.	Identifies a familiar object by touch when placed in a bag with 2 other objects. Uses "tomorrow," "yesterday." Figures out which child is missing by looking at children who are present. Asserts independence: "Me do it." Puts on simple garments such as cap or slippers.	When playing with a ring-stacking toy, ignores any forms that have no hole. Stacks only rings or other objects with holes. Classifies, labels, and sorts objects by group (hard versus soft, large versus small). Helps dress and undress self.	Frequently displays aggressive feelings and behaviors. Exhibits contrasting states and mood shifts (stubborn versus compliant). Shows increased fearfulness (dark, monsters, etc.). Expresses emotions with increasing control. Aware of own feelings and those of others. Shows pride in creation and production. Verbalizes feelings more often. Expresses feelings in symbolic play: Shows empathic concern for others.

For more information about programs for infants and toddlers:

Bell, S., & Ainsworth, M. D. S. (1972). Infant crying and maternal responsiveness. *Child Development, 43,* 1171–1190.

Brazelton, T. B. (1976). *Toddlers and parents: A declaration of independence.* New York: Dell.

Brazelton, T. B. (1983). *Infants and mothers: Differences in development.* New York: Delacorte.

Brazelton, T. B. (1983). *Working and caring.* Reading, MA: Addison-Wesley.

Brazelton, T. B. (1984). Cementing family relationships through child care. In L. Dittmann (Ed.), *The infants we care for* (rev. ed.). Washington, DC: NAEYC.

Brown, C. C. (Ed.). (1981). *Infants at risk: Assessment and intervention.* Skillman, NJ: Johnson & Johnson Baby Products Company Pediatric Round Table Series.

Cazden, C. (Ed.). (1981). *Language in early childhood education* (rev. ed.). Washington, DC: NAEYC.

Chance, P. (Ed.). (1979). *Learning through play.* Skillman, NJ: Johnson & Johnson Baby Products Company Pediatric Round Table Series.

Dittmann, L. (1984). *The infants we care for.* Washington, DC: NAEYC.

Erikson, E. (1950). *Childhood and society.* New York: Norton.

Fein, G., & Rivkin, M. (Eds.). (1986). *The young child at play: Reviews of research* (Vol. 4). Washington, DC: NAEYC.

Genishi, C. (1986). Acquiring language and communicative competence. In C. Seefeldt (Ed.), *Early childhood curriculum: A review of current research.* New York: Teachers College Press, Columbia University.

Gerber, M. (1982). What is appropriate curriculum for infants and toddlers? In B. Weissbourd & J. Musick (Eds.), *Infants: Their social environments.* Washington, DC: NAEYC.

Gonzalez-Mena, J. (1986). Toddlers: What to expect. *Young Children, 42*(1), 47–51.

Gonzalez-Mena, J., & Eyer, D. W. (1980). *Infancy and caregiving.* Palo Alto, CA: Mayfield.

Gordon, T. (1970). *Parent effectiveness training.* New York: Wyden.

Gordon, T. (1975). *Teacher effectiveness training.* New York: McKay.

Green, M. I. (1984). *A sign of relief.* Des Plaines, IL: Bantam.

Greenfield, P. M., & Tronick, E. (1980). *Infant curriculum, the Bromley-Health guide to the care of infants in groups.* Santa Monica, CA: Good Year Publishing.

Greenspan, S., & Greenspan, N. T. (1985). *First feelings: Milestones in the emotional development of your baby and child.* New York: Viking.

Hoffman, M. L. (1975). Moral internalization, parental power, and the nature of parent-child interaction. *Developmental Psychology, 11,* 228–239.

Honig, A. S. (1981). What are the needs of infants? *Young Children, 37*(1), 3–10.

Honig, A. S. (1982). Parent involvement in early childhood education. In B. Spodek (Ed.), *Handbook of research in early childhood education.* New York: Free Press.

Honig, A. S. (1985). High quality infant/toddler care. *Young Children, 41*(1), 40–46.

Honig, A. S., & Lally, R. (1981). *Infant caregiving: A design for training.* Syracuse, NY: Syracuse University Press.

Katz, L. (1980). Mothering and teaching: Some significant distinctions. In L. Katz (Ed.), *Current topics in early childhood education* (Vol. 3, pp. 47–64). Norwood, NJ: Ablex.

Kopp, C. B. (1982). Antecedents of self-regulation: A developmental perspective. *Developmental Psychology, 18,* 199–214.

Klaus, M. H., Leger, T., & Trause, M. A. (Eds.). (1975). *Maternal attachment and mothering disorders: A round table.* Skillman, NJ: Johnson & Johnson Baby Products Company Pediatric Round Table Series.

Klaus, M., & Robertson, M. O. (Eds.). (1982). *Birth, interaction and attachment.* Skillman, NJ: Johnson & Johnson Baby Products Company Pediatric Round Table Series.

Kuczynski, L. (1983). Reasoning, prohibitions, and motivations for compliance. *Developmental Psychology, 19,* 126–134.

Lansky, V. (1974). *Feed me! I'm yours.* Deephaven, MN: Meadowbrook.

Lightfoot, S. (1978). *Worlds apart: Relationships between families and schools.* New York: Basic.

Lozoff, B., Brillenham, G., Trause, M. A., Kennell, J. H., & Klaus, M. H. (1977). The mother-newborn relationship: Limits of adaptability. *Journal of Pediatrics, 91.*

McDonald, D. T. (1979). *Music in our lives: The early years.* Washington, DC: NAEYC.

Miller, C. S. (1984). Building self-control: Discipline for

young children. *Young Children, 40*(1), 15–19.

Moore, S. (1982). Prosocial behavior in the early years: Parent and peer influences. In B. Spodek (Ed.), *Handbook of research in early childhood education.* New York: Free Press.

Mussen, P., & Eisenberg-Bert, N. (1977). *Roots of caring, sharing, and helping: The development of prosocial behavior in children.* San Francisco: Freeman.

Piaget, J. (1950). *The psychology of intelligence.* London: Routledge & Kegan Paul.

Piaget, J. (1952). *The origins of intelligence in children.* (M. Cook, Trans.). New York: Norton. (Original work published 1936)

Princeton Center for Infancy. (1974). *The first twelve months of life: Your baby's growth month by month.* New York: Grosset & Dunlap.

Reilly, A. P. (Ed.). (1980). *The communication game.* Skillman, NJ: Johnson & Johnson Baby Products Company Pediatric Round Table Series.

Riley, S. S. (1984). *How to generate values in young children: Integrity, honesty, individuality, self-confidence.* Washington, DC: NAEYC.

Rogers, D. L., & Ross, D. D. (1986). Encouraging positive social interaction among young children. *Young Children, 41*(3), 12–17.

Rubin, K., & Everett, B. (1982). Social perspective-taking in young children. In S. G. Moore & C. R. Cooper (Eds.), *The young child: Reviews of research* (Vol. 3, pp. 97–114). Washington, DC: NAEYC.

Ruopp, R., Travers, J., Glantz, F., & Coelen, C. (1979). *Children at the center. Final report of the National Day Care Study* (Vol. 1). Cambridge, MA: Abt Associates.

Sackoff, E., & Hart, R. (1984, Summer). Toys: Research and applications. *Children's Environments Quarterly,* 1–2.

Sasserath, V. J., & Hoekelman, R. A. (1983). *Child health care communications.* Skillman, NJ: Johnson & Johnson Baby Products Company Pediatric Round Table Series.

Schachter, F. F., & Strage, A. A. (1982). Adults' talk and children's language development. In S. G. Moore & C. R. Cooper (Eds.), *The young child: Reviews of research* (Vol. 3, pp. 79–96). Washington, DC: NAEYC.

Schaffer, H. R. (1984). *The child's entry into a social world.* Orlando, FL: Academic.

Schickedanz, J. (1986). *More than the ABCs: The early stages of reading and writing.* Washington, DC: NAEYC.

Schickedanz, J., Schickedanz, D. I., & Forsyth, P. D. (1982). *Toward understanding children.* Boston: Little, Brown.

Segal, M. (1974). *From birth to one year.* Fort Lauderdale: Nova University.

Segal, M., & Adcock, D. (1976). *From one to two years.* Fort Lauderdale: Nova University.

Smith, C. A., & Davis, D. E. (1976). Teaching children non-sense. *Young Children, 34*(3), 4–11.

Sparling, J. (1984). *Learning games for the first three years.* New York: Walker.

Sprung, B. (1978). *Perspectives on non-sexist early childhood education.* New York: Teachers College Press, Columbia University.

Sroufe, L. A. (1979). The coherence of individual development. *American Psychologist, 34,* 834–841.

Stewart, I. S. (1982). The real world of teaching two-year-old children. *Young Children, 37*(5), 3–13.

Stone, J. G. (1978). *A guide to discipline* (rev. ed.). Washington, DC: NAEYC.

Thoman, E. B., & Trotter, S. (Eds.). (1978). *Social responsiveness of infants.* Skillman, NJ: Johnson & Johnson Baby Products Company Pediatric Round Table Series.

Warren, R. M. (1977). *Caring: Supporting children's growth.* Washington, DC: NAEYC.

Weissbourd, B. (1981). Supporting parents as people. In B. Weissbourd & J. Musick (Eds.), *Infants: Their social environments.* Washington, DC: NAEYC.

Wellman, H. M. (1982). The foundations of knowledge: Concept development in the young child. In S. G. Moore & C. R. Cooper (Eds.), *The young child: Reviews of research* (Vol. 3, pp. 115–134). Washington, DC: NAEYC.

White, B. (1975). *The first three years of life.* Englewood Cliffs, NJ: Prentice-Hall.

Willis, A., & Ricciuti, H. (1975). *A good beginning for babies: Guidelines for group care.* Washington, DC: NAEYC.

Integrated Components of Developmentally Appropriate Practice for Infants and Toddlers

---

In Part 2 of this book, the National Center for Clinical Infant Programs and NAEYC describe the vital development that takes place during the first 3 years of life and give examples of appropriate care of infants and toddlers. Building on the previous description of development and practice, Part 3 is designed for practitioners who care for infants or toddlers in group settings. Both appropriate and inappropriate practices are described here, because people often understand a concept most clearly if they are presented both positive and negative examples.

Because all areas of development are thoroughly integrated during early childhood, the title for these descriptions refers to integrated components. The components of practice that are referred to in this section parallel the components of a group program as described in NAEYC's Accreditation Criteria and Procedures of the National Academy of Early Childhood Programs. It is hoped that the descriptions of appropriate and inappropriate practices that follow will help directors and teachers to interpret and apply the accreditation Criteria to their work with infants and toddlers.

Because development is so individual, these statements do not define infants and toddlers by chronological age. For the purpose of clarity, the infant statement is directed toward the care of non-walking children and the toddler statement addresses caring for children from the time they are walking until they are between 2½ and 3-years-old.

Integrated Components of APPROPRIATE and INAPPROPRIATE Practice for *INFANTS*

Component	APPROPRIATE Practice	INAPPROPRIATE Practice
Interactions among adults and children	• Adults engage in many one-to-one, face-to-face interactions with infants. Adults talk in a pleasant, soothing voice, and use simple language and frequent eye contact.	• Infants are left for long periods in cribs, playpens, or seats without adult attention. Adults are harsh, shout, or use baby talk.
	• Infants are held and carried frequently to provide them with a wide variety of experiences. The adults talk to the infant before, during, and after moving the infant around.	• Infants are wordlessly moved about at the adult's convenience. Nothing is explained to infants.
	• Adults are especially attentive to infants during routines such as diaper changing, feeding, and changing clothes. The caregiver explains what will happen, what is happening, and what will happen next.	• Routines are swiftly accomplished without involving the infant. Little or no warm interactions take place during routines.
	• All interactions are characterized by gentle, supportive responses. Adults listen and respond to sounds that infants make, imitate them, and respect infants' sounds as the beginning of communication.	• Adults are rough, harsh, or ignore the child's responses.

Component	APPROPRIATE Practice	INAPPROPRIATE Practice
Interactions among adults and children (*continued*)	• Caregivers respond quickly to infants' cries or calls of distress, recognizing that crying and body movements are infants' only way to communicate. Responses are soothing and tender.	• Crying is ignored or responded to irregularly at the convenience of the adult. Crying is treated as a nuisance. Adults' responses neglect the infants' needs.
	• Playful interactions with babies are done in ways that are sensitive to the child's level of tolerance for physical movement, louder sounds, or other changes.	• Adults frighten, tease, or upset children with their unpredictable behaviors.
	• Children's play interests are respected. Adults observe the child's activity and comment, offer additional ideas for play, and encourage the child's engagement in the activity.	• Infants are interrupted, toys are whisked from their grasp, adults impose their own ideas or even play with toys themselves regardless of the child's interest.
	• The caregiver frequently talks with, sings to, and reads to infants. Language is a vital, lively form of communication with individuals.	• Infants are expected to entertain themselves or watch television. Language is used infrequently and vocabularies limited.
	• Infants and their parents are greeted warmly and with enthusiasm each morning. The caregiver holds the baby upon arrival and gradually helps the child become a part of the small group.	• Babies are placed on the floor or in a crib with no caregiver interaction. Caregivers receive children coldly and without individual attention.
	• Caregivers consistently respond to infants' needs for food and comfort thus enabling the infants to develop trust in the adults who care for them, so they find the world a secure place to be.	• Adults are unpredictable and/or unresponsive. They act as if children are a bother.
	• Caregivers adjust to infants' individual feeding and sleeping schedules. Their food preferences and eating styles are respected.	• Schedules are rigid and based on adults' rather than children's needs. Food is used for rewards (or denied as punishment).
	• Infants are praised for their accomplishments and helped to feel increasingly competent.	• Infants are criticized for what they cannot do or for their clumsy struggle to master a skill. They are made to feel inadequate and that they have no effect on others.
	• Teachers respect infants' curiosity about each other. At the same time, adults help ensure that children treat each other gently.	• Infants are not allowed to touch each other gently, or are forced to share or play together when they have no interest in doing so.
	• Adults model the type of interactions with others that they want children to develop.	• Adults are aggressive, shout, or exhibit a lack of coping behaviors under stress.
	• Adults frequently engage in games such as Peek-a-Boo and 5 Little Piggies with infants who are interested and responsive to the play.	• Games are imposed on children regardless of their interest. Play is seen as a time filler rather than a learning experience.

Component	APPROPRIATE Practice	INAPPROPRIATE Practice
Interactions among adults and children (*continued*)	• Diaper changing, feeding, and other routines are viewed as vital learning experiences for babies.	• Routines are dealt with superficially and indifferently.
	• Healthy, accepting attitudes about children's bodies and their functions are expressed.	• Infants are made to feel their bodies are not to be touched or admired, and that bodily functions are disgusting.
Environment	• The diapering, sleeping, feeding, and play areas are separate to ensure sanitation and provide quiet, restful areas.	• Areas are combined and are very noisy and distracting.
	• The environment contains both soft (pillows, padded walls) and hard (rocking chair, mirrors) elements.	• The environment is either sterile or cluttered, but lacks variety.
	• Babies find contrasts in color and design interesting, so bright colors are used to create distinct patterns.	• Rooms are sterile and bland.
	• Children have their own cribs, bedding, feeding utensils, clothing, diapers, pacifiers, and other special comforting objects. Infants' names are used to label every personal item.	• Infants share sleeping quarters in shifts, or otherwise do not have their own special supplies.
	• The area that is the focus of play changes periodically during the day from the floor, to strollers, to being carried, to rocking or swinging, and other variations to give infants different perspectives on people and places. Children are cared for both indoors and outdoors.	• Babies are confined to cribs, playpens, or the floor for long periods indoors. Time outdoors is viewed as too much bother, or is not done because of excuses about the weather.
	• Mirrors are placed where infants can observe themselves—on the wall next to the floor, next to the diapering area.	• Children never have a chance to see themselves.
	• Fresh air and healthy heat/humidity/cooling conditions are maintained.	• Rooms are too hot or too cold.
	• The room is cheerful and decorated at children's eye level with pictures of people's faces, friendly animals, and other familiar objects. Pictures of children and their families are displayed.	• Areas are dingy and dark. Decorations are at adult eye level and are uninteresting. No family photos are displayed.
	• A variety of music is provided for enjoyment in listening/body movement/singing.	• Music is used to distract or lull infants to sleep. Children hear only children's songs.
	• Space is arranged so children can enjoy moments of quiet play by themselves, so they have space to roll over, and so they can crawl toward interesting objects.	• Space is cramped and unsafe for children who are learning how to move their bodies.
	• Floors are covered by easy-to-clean carpet. Infants are barefoot whenever possible.	• Floor coverings are dirty or hard and cold. Infants must wear shoes.

Component	APPROPRIATE Practice	INAPPROPRIATE Practice
Equipment	• Toys are safe, washable, and too large for infants to swallow. They range from very simple to more complex.	• Toys are sharp, tiny, with chipping paint, or otherwise unsafe and not washable. Toys are too simple or too complex for the infants served.
	• Toys provided are responsive to the child's actions: bells, busy boards, balls, vinyl-covered pillows to climb on, large beads that snap together, nesting bowls, small blocks, shape sorters, music boxes, squeeze toys that squeak.	• Toys are battery-powered or wind up so the baby just watches. Toys lack a variety of texture, size, and shape.
	• Mobiles are designed to be seen from the child's viewpoint. They are removed when children can reach for and grasp them.	• Mobiles are out of infants' vision. They are positioned where children can reach them.
	• Toys are scaled to a size that enables infants to grasp, chew, and manipulate them (clutch balls, rattles, spoons, teethers, rubber dolls).	• Toys are too large to handle, or unsafe for children to chew on.
	• Toys are available on open shelves so children can make their own selections.	• Toys are dumped in a box or kept out of children's reach forcing them to depend on adults' selection.
	• Low climbing structures and steps are provided. Structures are well padded and safe for exploration.	• No provisions are made for children to climb, or structures are only safe for older, more mobile children.
	• Books are heavy cardboard with rounded edges. They have bright pictures of familiar objects.	• Books are not available, or are made of paper that tears easily. Books do not contain objects familiar or interesting to children. Faded colors or intricate drawings are used.
	• Pictorial materials depict a variety of ages and ethnic groups in a positive way.	• Pictures are limited to cartoon characters or stereotypes.
Health, safety, and nutrition	• Health and safety precautions are taken to limit the spread of infectious disease. Toys that are mouthed are replaced when a child has finished with them so they can be cleaned with a bleach solution.	• Toys are scattered on the floor and cleaned occasionally, not at all, or improperly. Bottles sit on the floor. Spills are ignored.
	• Written records are maintained for each child. Immunizations are current. Up-to-date emergency information is readily available.	• Written records are incomplete or outdated.
	• Staff are in good health and take precautions not to spread infection.	• Because of limited sick leave, staff come to work even when they are ill.
	• Children are always under adult supervision.	• Children are left unattended.
	• The environment is safe for children—electrical outlets are covered, no hazardous substances are within children's reach, no extension cords are exposed.	• Children are frequently told "no" to hazards that should be removed. Rocking chairs are placed in crawling areas.

Component	APPROPRIATE Practice	INAPPROPRIATE Practice
Health, safety, and nutrition (*continued*)	• Children are dressed appropriately for the weather and type of play they engage in.	• Infants' clothing is too confining, uncomfortable, or difficult to manage. Infants are over- or under-dressed.
	• Adults wash their hands before and after each diaper change, before and after feeding each infant.	• Adults are too casual or inconsistent about handwashing.
	• Adults are aware of the symptoms of common illnesses, environmental hazards such as lead poisoning, and food or other allergies.	• Staff do not notice or ignore changes in children's normal behavior or do not know children well enough to detect unusual behavior.
	• Diaper changing areas are easily and routinely sanitized after each change.	• Several children are changed on the same surface without sanitizing it for each child.
	• Children are always held with their bodies at an angle when being fed from a bottle.	• Bottles are propped up for children or children are left lying down with a bottle.
	• Children who can sit up eat in groups of one or two with a caregiver to ensure adult assistance as needed. Finger foods are encouraged. Only healthy foods are fed. Eating is considered a sociable, happy time.	• Large groups of children are fed in sequence or left to their own devices. Cookies and other sugary foods are used as treats. Children are not allowed to mess with their food. Conversation is limited.
Staff-parent interactions	• Parents are viewed as the child's primary source of affection and care. Staff support parents and work with them to help them feel confident as parents.	• Staff feel in competition with parents. They avoid controversial issues rather than resolving them with parents.
	• Parents and staff talk daily to share pertinent information about the child.	• Staff rarely talk with parents except at planned conferences.
	• Staff help parents anticipate the child's next areas of development and prepare them to support the child.	• Staff fail to provide parents with information or insights to help them do what is best for their child.
Staff qualifications	• Staff enjoy working with infants and are warmly responsive to their needs. Staff have had training specifically related to infant development and caregiving. They know what skills and behaviors emerge during the first few months, and support children as they become increasingly competent and knowledgeable. Staff are competent in first aid.	• Staff view work with infants as a chore and as custodial in nature. Staff have little or no training specific to infant development. They have unrealistic expectations for this age group. They are unaware of what to look for that might signal problems in development.
Staffing	• The group size and ratio of adults to infants is limited to allow for one-to-one interaction, intimate knowledge of individual babies, and consistent caregiving. Babies need to relate to the same, very few people each day. A ratio of 1 adult to no more than 3 infants is best.	• Group size and staff-child ratio are too large to permit individual attention and constant supervision. Staffing patterns require infants to relate to more than 2 different adults during the caregiving day.

Lois Main

Adults must be especially careful to give toddlers many chances to figure things out for themselves, while remaining available to them if they ask for assistance.

Subjects & Predicates

When children direct their own play, they see themselves as competent people.

39

Integrated Components of
APPROPRIATE and INAPPROPRIATE Practice for
TODDLERS

Component	APPROPRIATE Practice	INAPPROPRIATE Practice
Interactions among adults and children	• Adults engage in many one-to-one, face-to-face conversations with toddlers. Adults let toddlers initiate language, and wait for a response, even from children whose language is limited. Adults label or name objects, describe events, and reflect feelings to help children learn new words. Adults simplify their language for toddlers who are just beginning to talk (instead of "It's time to wash our hands and have snack," the adult says, "Let's wash hands. Snack-time!") Then as children acquire their own words, adults expand on the toddler's language (for example, *Toddler*— "Mary sock." *Adult*—"Oh, that's Mary's missing sock and you found it.").	• Adults talk *at* toddlers and do not wait for a response. Adult voices dominate or adults do not speak to children because they think they are too young to respond. Adults either talk "baby talk" or use language that is too complex for toddlers to understand.
	• Adults are supportive of toddlers as they acquire skills. Adults watch to see what the child is trying to do and provide the necessary support to help the child accomplish the task, allowing children to do what they are capable of doing and assisting with tasks that are frustrating.	• Adults are impatient and intrusive. They expect too much or too little of toddlers. Because it is faster, adults do tasks for toddlers that children can do themselves. Or adults allow children to become frustrated by tasks they cannot do.
	• Adults respond quickly to toddlers' cries or calls for help, recognizing that toddlers have limited language with which to communicate their needs.	• Crying is ignored or responded to irregularly or at the adults' convenience.
	• Adults respect children's developing preferences for familiar objects, foods, and people. Adults permit children to keep their own favorite objects and provide limited options from which children may choose what they prefer to eat or wear. Children's preferences are seen as a healthy indication of a developing self-concept.	• Adults prohibit favored objects like blankets or toys or arbitrarily take them away or expect toddlers to share them with other children. Children are not given choices and preferences are not encouraged. Children are all expected to do the same thing.
	• Adults respect toddlers' desire to carry favored objects around with them, to move objects like household items from one place to another, and to roam around or sit and parallel play with toys and objects.	• Adults restrict objects to certain locations and do not tolerate hoarding, collecting, or carrying.

Component	APPROPRIATE Practice	INAPPROPRIATE Practice
Interactions among adults and children (*continued*)	• Adults patiently redirect toddlers to help guide children toward controlling their own impulses and behavior. When children fight over the same toy, the adult provides another like it or removes the toy. If neither of these strategies is effective, the adult may gently remove the toddler and redirect the child's attention by initiating play in another area. Adults only punish children for overtly dangerous behavior.	• Adults ignore disputes leading to a chaotic atmosphere or punish infractions harshly, frightening and humiliating children.
	• Adults recognize that constantly testing limits and expressing opposition to adults ("NO!") is part of developing a healthy sense of self as a separate, autonomous individual. Adults only say "No" when the prohibition relates to children's safety. Adults give positively worded directions ("Bang on the floor") not just restrictions ("Don't bang on the table").	• Adults are constantly saying "No!" to toddlers or becoming involved in power struggles over issues that do not relate to the child's health or well-being. Adults punish children for asserting themselves or saying "No."
	• Children are praised for their accomplishments and helped to feel increasingly competent and in control of themselves.	• Toddlers are criticized for what they cannot do or for their clumsy struggle to master a skill. Or adults foster dependency; children are overprotected and made to feel inadequate.
	• Children and their parents are greeted warmly and with enthusiasm each morning. The day begins with a great deal of adult-child contact. Adults help toddlers settle into the group by reading books or quietly playing with them.	• Children are received coldly and given no individual attention. Toddlers are expected to begin the day with free play and little adult supervision.
	• Adults model the type of interactions with others that they want children to develop. Adults recognize that most of the time when toddlers are aggressive, hurting or biting other children, it is because they lack skills to cope with frustrating situations such as wanting another child's toy. Adults model for toddlers the words to say ("Susan, I want the jack-in-the-box now") or redirect them to another activity.	• Adults are aggressive, shout, or exhibit a lack of coping behaviors under stress. Adult attempts to punish or control the aggressive toddler escalate the hostility.
Living and learning with toddlers (curriculum)	• Adults recognize that routine tasks of living like eating, toileting, and dressing are important opportunities to help children learn about their world and to regulate their own behavior.	• Routine times are chaotic because all children are expected to do the same thing at the same time.

Component	APPROPRIATE Practice	INAPPROPRIATE Practice
Living and learning with toddlers (curriculum) (*continued*)	• Adults play with toddlers reciprocally, modeling for toddlers how to play imaginatively with baby dolls and accessories. For example, adults and children play "tea party" where the adult pretends to drink from a cup and exclaims how good it tastes and then the toddler often models the adult.	• Adults do not play with toddlers because they feel silly or bored.
	• Adults support toddlers' play so that toddlers stay interested in an object or activity for longer periods of time and their play becomes more complex, moving from simple awareness and exploration of objects to more complicated play like pretending.	• Adults do not think that supporting children's play is important. They do not understand the value of play for learning or they feel silly playing with young children.
	• Toddlers' solitary and parallel play is respected. Adults provide several of the same popular toys for children to play with alone or near another child. Adults realize that having three or four of the same sought-after toy is more helpful than having one each of many different toys.	• Adults do not understand the value of solitary and parallel play and try to force children to play together. Adults arbitrarily expect children to share. Popular toys are not provided in duplicate and fought over constantly while other toys are seldom used.
	• Adults prepare the environment to allow for predictability and repetition, as well as events that can be expected and anticipated.	• Adults lose patience with doing many of the same things repeatedly and get bored by toddlers' needs to repeat tasks until they master them or feel secure in a predictable environment.
	• Adults frequently read to toddlers, individually on laps or in groups of two or three. Adults sing with toddlers, do fingerplays, act out simple stories like "The Three Bears" with children participating actively, or tell stories using a flannelboard or magnetic board, and allow children to manipulate and place figures on the boards.	• Adults impose "group time" on toddlers, forcing a large group to listen or watch an activity without opportunity for children to participate.
	• Toddlers are given appropriate art media such as large crayons, watercolor markers, and large paper. Adults expect toddlers to explore and manipulate art materials and do *not* expect them to produce a finished art product. Adults *never* use food for art because toddlers are developing self-regulatory skills and must learn to distinguish between food and other objects that are not to be eaten.	• Toddlers are "helped" by teachers to produce a product, follow the adult-made model, or color a coloring book or ditto sheet. Tactilely sensitive toddlers are required to fingerpaint or are given edible fingerpaint or playdough because they will probably put it in their mouths.

Component	APPROPRIATE Practice	INAPPROPRIATE Practice
Living and learning with toddlers (curriculum) (*continued*)	• Time schedules are flexible and smooth, dictated more by children's needs than by adults. There is a relatively predictable sequence to the day to help children feel secure.	• Activities are dictated by rigid adherence to time schedules or the lack of any time schedule makes the day unpredictable.
	• Children's schedules are respected with regard to eating and sleeping. Toddlers are provided snacks more frequently and in smaller portions than older children. For example, 2 morning snacks are offered at earlier hours than are usually provided for preschoolers. Liquids are provided frequently. Children's food preferences are respected.	• Schedules are rigid and based on adults' rather than children's needs. Food is used for rewards or withheld as punishment. Children are allowed to become fussy and cranky waiting for food that is served on a rigid schedule.
	• Diaper changing, toilet learning, eating, dressing, and other routines are viewed as vital learning experiences.	• Routines are dealt with superficially and indifferently.
	• Children learn to use the toilet through consistent, positive encouragement by adults. When toddlers reach an age where they feel confident and unafraid to sit a potty seat, adults invite them to use the potty, help them as needed, provide manageable clothing, and positively reinforce their behavior regardless of the outcome. Children are provided a toddler-appropriate potty seat and step-stool, if needed, in a well-lit, inviting, relatively private space. Children are taken to the toilet frequently and regularly in response to their own biological habits. Toddlers are never scolded or shamed about toileting or wet diapers/pants.	• Toilet learning is imposed on children to meet the adults' needs, whether children are ready or not. Children are made to sit on the potty for undue lengths of time and only reinforced contingent on urinating or defecating in the potty. Children are punished or shamed for toileting accidents.
	• Healthy, accepting attitudes about children's bodies and their functions are expressed.	• Children are made to feel their bodies are not to be to admired, and that bodily functions are disgusting.
	• Children have daily opportunities for exploratory activity outdoors, such as water and sand play and easel painting. Waterplay is available daily, requiring that adults dry clothes or provide clothing changes. Children have opportunities for supervised play in sand. Adults recognize that sand is a soft and absorbing medium ideally suited for toddler exploration. Well-supervised sand play is used to teach children to self-regulate what they can and cannot eat.	• Adults do not offer water and sand play because they are messy and require supervision, using as an excuse that children will get wet or will eat sand. Children's natural enjoyment of water play is frustrated so they play in toilets or at sinks whenever they can.

Component	APPROPRIATE Practice	INAPPROPRIATE Practice
Living and learning with toddlers (curriculum) (*continued*)	• Routines are planned as learning experiences to help children become skilled and independent. Meals and snacks include finger food or utensils that are easier for toddlers to use such as bowls, spoons, and graduated versions of drinking objects from bottles to cups. Dressing and undressing are seen as learning activities and children's attempts to dress themselves and put on shoes are supported and positively encouraged.	• Adults foster children's dependence by doing routine tasks for them that they could do for themselves. Children feel incompetent because the eating utensils are too difficult for them or clothes require adult assistance with tiny buttons or laces.
	• Food is ready before children are called to meals so they do not have to wait.	• Hungry toddlers become frustrated and cranky when they are set up to eat and then must wait to be served.
Environment	• The diapering/toileting, sleeping, feeding, and play areas are separate both for sanitation and to ensure quiet, restful areas.	• Areas are combined and very noisy and distracting.
	• The environment contains both soft (pillows, padded walls, carpeting) and hard (rocking chairs, mirrors) elements.	• The environment is dominated by hard surfaces because they are easier to keep clean.
	• The environment contains private spaces with room for no more than 2 children.	• The environment provides no private spaces.
	• Children have their own cribs or cots, bedding, feeding utensils, clothing, and other special comforting objects. Toddlers' names are used to label every personal item.	• Children share sleeping quarters in shifts, or otherwise do not have their own special supplies. Favored objects are not permitted.
	• Children have many opportunities for active, large muscle play both indoors and outdoors. The environment includes ramps and steps that are the correct size for children to practice newly acquired skills. Toddlers' outdoor play space is separate from that of older children. Outdoor play equipment for toddlers includes small climbing equipment that they can go around, in, and out of, and solitary play equipment requiring supervision such as swings and low slides.	• Toddlers' indoor space is cramped and unsafe for children who are just learning how to move their bodies and need to run more than walk. Toddlers share outdoor space and unsafe equipment designed for older children.
	• The room is cheerful and decorated at the children's eye level with pictures of faces of people, friendly animals, and other familiar objects. Pictures of children and their families are encouraged.	• Areas are dingy and dark. Decorations are at adult eye levels, or are too syrupy and cute. No evidence exists of personal involvement for families.

Component	APPROPRIATE Practice	INAPPROPRIATE Practice
Environment (*continued*)	• Sturdy picture books are provided. Pictures depict a variety of ages and ethnic groups in a positive way. • Toys are available on open shelves so children can make their own selections. Toys can be carried and moved about in the environment as children choose. • Climbing structures and steps are low, well-padded, and safe for exploration.	• Books are not available because they get torn or soiled. Pictures are cartoons or other stereotypes. • Toys are dumped in a box or kept away from children's reach so they are at the mercy of the adult's selection. Adults attempt to restrict the use of toys to certain areas, like housekeeping or blocks. • No provisions are made for children to climb, or structures are safe only for older, more mobile children.
Health, safety, and nutrition	• Health and safety precautions are taken to limit the spread of infectious disease. Toys that are mouthed are replaced when a child has finished with them so they can be cleaned with a bleach solution. • Written records are maintained for each child. Immunizations are current. Up-to-date emergency information is readily available. • Staff are in good health and take precautions not to spread infection. • Children are always under adult supervision. • The environment is safe for children—electrical outlets are covered, no hazardous substances are within children's reach, no extension cords are exposed. • Children are dressed appropriately for the weather and type of play they engage in. • Adults wash their hands before and after each diaper change, before and after assisting children with toileting, and before handling food. • Adults are aware of the symptoms of common illnesses, alert to changes in children's behavior that may signal illness or allergies. • Diaper changing areas are easily and routinely sanitized after each change.	• Toys are scattered on the floor and cleaned occasionally, not at all, or improperly. • Written records are incomplete or outdated. • Because of limited or no sick leave, staff come to work even when they are ill. • Children are left unattended. • Children are frequently told "no" to hazards that should be removed. • Toddlers' clothing is too confining, uncomfortable, or difficult to manage. • Adults are inconsistent or too casual about handwashing. • Staff do not notice or ignore changes in children's behavior or do not know children well enough to detect changes in normal patterns of behavior. • Several children are changed on the same surface.
Staff-parent interactions	• Parents are viewed as the child's primary source of affection and care. Staff support parents and work with them to help them feel confident as parents.	• Staff feel in competition with parents. They avoid controversial issues rather than resolving them with parents.

Component	APPROPRIATE Practice	INAPPROPRIATE Practice
Staff-parent interactions (*continued*)	• Parents and staff talk daily to share pertinent information about the child. There is an established system for keeping records of children's daily activity and health and reporting to parents. • Staff help parents anticipate the child's next areas of development and prepare them to support the child.	• Staff rarely talk with parents except at planned conferences. • Staff fail to provide parents with information or insights to help them do what is best for their child.
Staff qualifications	• Staff enjoy working with toddlers, are warmly responsive to their needs, and demonstrate considerable patience in supporting children as they become increasingly competent and independent. Staff have training in child development and early education specific to the toddler age group. Staff are competent in first aid.	• Staff view work with toddlers as a chore and as custodial in nature. They push children to achieve and are impatient with their struggles, or they expect too little of toddlers. They are unaware of what to look for that might signal problems in development. Staff have no training in child development/early education or their training and experience are limited to working with older children.
Staffing	• The group size and ratio of adults to children is limited to allow for the intimate, interpersonal atmosphere, and high level of supervision toddlers require. Maximum group size is 12 with 1 adult for no more than 6 toddlers, preferably fewer. Staffing patterns limit the number of different adults toddlers relate to each day.	• Group size and staff-child ratio are too large to allow for individual attention and close supervision. Staff contain the chaos rather than respond to and support individual development. Staffing patterns require toddlers to relate to several different adults who do not know them well.

In a good program, adults respect children's choice to share only when the children are willing to do so.

Subjects & Predicates

46

PART 4

Developmentally Appropriate Practice in Programs for 3-Year-Olds

The 3-year-old is sometimes overlooked when periods of development are described in broad categories like "toddlers" or "preschoolers." But the fourth year of life is a distinct period of development with its own unique challenges and accomplishments. Teachers in programs serving 3-year-olds, as in all early childhood programs, must consider what is appropriate for this age group in general as well as what is specifically appropriate for the individual children in their care.

Three-year-olds are no longer toddlers but they will behave like toddlers at times; at other times their language ability and motor skills will deceptively mimic the 4-year-old. The key for the teacher of 3s is to maintain appropriate expectations; teachers should not expect too little of 3-year-olds, nor should they expect too much. To care for and educate a group of 3s, teachers need to fully understand the developmental continuum from toddlerhood through the preschool years. At 2½, many children begin to display skills and behaviors most typical of 3-year-olds. Thus, children between 2½ and 3½ years of age are often similar developmentally; and some 3½-year-olds share traits of 4s. The common practice of multiage grouping, putting children of a wide age span together, further necessitates that teachers fully understand the continuum of development during the early years.

The following statement describes some developmentally appropriate and inappropriate practices specifically related to 3-year-olds. *This statement is not intended to describe a comprehensive program for 3s. It is intended to be used with the statement on appropriate practice for toddlers (pages 40–46) and the statement on appropriate practice for 4- and 5-year-olds (pages 51–59).*

Living and Learning With 3-Year-Olds: Interactions Among Adults and Children and Appropriate Curriculum

APPROPRIATE Practice	INAPPROPRIATE Practice
• Adults provide affection and support, comforting children when they cry and reassuring them when fearful. Adults plan experiences to alleviate children's fears.	• Adults are cold or distant and do not express physical affection, comfort, or emotional bolstering. Adults assume children will get over fears.
• Adults support 3-year-olds' play and developing independence, helping when needed, but allowing them to do what they are capable of doing and what they want to do for themselves ("I can do it myself!").	• Adults expect 3-year-olds to be independent and to entertain themselves for long periods of time; they are impatient, hurry children, and do tasks for children that they could do themselves.
• Adults recognize that, although 3-year-olds are usually more cooperative than toddlers and want to please adults, they may revert to toddler behavior (thumb-sucking, crying, hitting, baby talk) when they are feeling shy or upset, especially in a new situation. Adults know that 3-year-olds' interest in babies, and especially their own recent infancy, is an opportunity for children to learn about themselves and human development.	• Adults expect too much of 3-year-olds and ridicule them when they behave immaturely or play baby ("You're acting like a baby!").

APPROPRIATE Practice

- Adults provide opportunities for 3-year-olds to demonstrate and practice their newly developed self-help skills and their desire to help adults with dressing and undressing, toileting, feeding themselves (including helping with pouring milk or setting the table), brushing teeth, washing hands, and helping pick up toys. Adults are patient with occasional toileting accidents, spilled food, and unfinished jobs.

- Adults know that growth rates may slow down and appetites decrease at this age. Children are encouraged to eat "tastes" in small portions with the possibility of more servings if desired.

- Adults guide 3-year-olds to take naps or do restful activities periodically throughout the day, recognizing that these younger children may exhaust themselves—especially when trying to keep up with older children in the group.

- Adults provide many opportunities for 3s to play by themselves, next to another child (parallel play), or with one or two other children. Adults recognize that 3-year-olds are not comfortable with much group participation. Adults read a story or play music with small groups and allow children to enter and leave the group at will.

- Adults support children's beginning friendships, recognizing that such relationships ("my best friend") are short-lived and may consist of acting silly together or chasing for a few minutes. When conflicts arise, the 3-year-old will often return to playing alone. Adults encourage children to take turns and share but do not always expect children to give up favored items.

- Adults provide plenty of space and time indoors and outdoors for children to explore and exercise their large muscle skills like running, jumping, galloping, riding a tricycle, or catching a ball, with adults close by to offer assistance as needed.

- Adults provide large amounts of uninterrupted time for children to persist at self-chosen tasks and activities and to practice and perfect their newly developed physical skills if they choose.

INAPPROPRIATE Practice

- Adults perform routine tasks (like dressing and cleaning up) for children because it is faster and less messy. Adults punish or shame children for toileting accidents and do not allow children to play with their food. Adults insist that children pick up all the toys every time.

- Adults serve children a large meal which they are expected to eat. Disciplinary pressures accompany demands for food consumption.

- Naptime is either forced or not provided. Children are scolded for being cranky or tired as the day progresses.

- Adults expect children to participate in whole group activities. They read a story to all the children at once, expecting them all to sit and listen quietly. They do not allow children to leave the large group activity.

- Adults expect that children will always want to play with their "friends" and require that they do activities together or share toys. Adults pick out friends for children and keep pairs together over time.

- Adults restrict children's physical activity ("No running!") or provide limited space and little equipment for large muscle outdoor activity. Adults limit large muscle activity to a short outdoor recess time.

- Adults become impatient with children who want to repeat a task or activity again and again, OR they force children to repeat tasks that adults have selected as learning activities whether the child is interested or not.

APPROPRIATE Practice	**INAPPROPRIATE Practice**

- Adults provide many materials and opportunities for children to develop fine motor skills such as puzzles, pegboards, beads to string, construction sets, and art materials (crayons, brushes, paints, markers, play dough, blunt scissors). Although children's scribbles are more controlled than those of toddlers, and 3-year-olds will create designs with horizontal and vertical strokes, and will sometimes name their drawings and paintings, adults do not expect a representational product. Art is viewed as creative expression and exploration of materials.

- Adults provide plenty of materials and time for children to explore and learn about the environment, to exercise their natural curiosity, and to experiment with cause and effect relationships. For example, they provide blocks (that children line up first and later may build into towers); more complex dramatic play props (for playing work and family roles and animals); sand and water with tools for pouring, measuring, and scooping; many toys and tools to experiment with like knobs, latches, and any toy that opens, closes, and can be taken apart; and simple science activities like blowing bubbles, flying kites, or planting seeds.

- Adults encourage children's developing language by speaking clearly and frequently to individual children and listening to their response. Adults respond quickly and appropriately to children's verbal initiatives. They recognize that talking may be more important than listening for 3-year-olds. Adults patiently answer children's questions ("Why?" "How come?") and recognize that 3-year-olds often ask questions they know the answers to in order to open a discussion or practice giving answers themselves. Adults know that children are rapidly acquiring language, experimenting with verbal sounds, and beginning to use language to solve problems and learn concepts.

- Adults provide many experiences and opportunities to extend children's language and musical abilities. Adults read books to one child or a small group; recite simple poems, nursery rhymes and finger plays; encourage children to sing songs and listen to recordings; facilitate children's play of circle and movement games like London Bridge, Farmer in the Dell, and Ring Around the Rosie; provide simple rhythm instruments; listen to stories that children tell or write down stories they dictate; and enjoy 3-year-olds' sense of humor.

- Adults expect children to demonstrate fine motor skills by cutting out figures or shapes, by coloring within the lines in coloring books or on ditto sheets, or following the teacher's directions and model to create identical art products. When children draw or paint pictures, teachers ask "What is it?" and lead children to believe that only a representational picture is valued.

- Adults may provide blocks and dramatic play areas but have definite ideas about how these areas should be used and restrict materials to the designated area of the room. Water play and sand play are not provided because they are too messy and difficult to supervise. Adults do not provide toys and tools to use in take-apart activities because they require too much time to clean up.

- Adults attempt to maintain quiet in the classroom and punish children who talk too much. Adults speak to the whole group most of the time and only speak to individual children to admonish or discipline them. Adults ridicule children's asking of rhetorical questions by saying, "Oh, you know that."

- Adults limit language and music activities because children sometimes become too silly or loud, OR they include story time and music time only as a whole group activity and require children to participate. Adults discipline children for using silly or nonsense language.

49

APPROPRIATE Practice

- Adults know that 3-year-olds do not usually understand or remember the rules. Guidance reasons that are specific to a real situation and that are demonstrated repeatedly are more likely to impress young children.
- Adults provide a safe, hazard-free environment and careful supervision. Adults recognize that 3-year-olds often overestimate their newly developed physical powers and will try activities that are unsafe or beyond their ability (especially in multiage groups where they may model 4- and 5-year-olds). Adults protect children's safety in these situations while also helping them deal with their frustration and maintain their self-confidence ("Joel can tie his shoe because he's 5; when you're 5, you'll probably know how to tie, too.").

INAPPROPRIATE Practice

- Adults expect children to remember and abide by a list of classroom rules. Children are scolded and belittled for not remembering and applying a rule.

- Adults are careless about supervision especially when 3-year-olds are in a group of mostly 4- and 5-year-olds who are capable of more self-monitoring and control of their own bodies.

Bibliography

Elkind, D. (1974). *A sympathetic understanding of the child: Birth to sixteen.* Boston: Allyn & Bacon.

Holt, B., & Karas, S. (1986). *Iowa family day care handbook* (3rd ed.). Ames, IA: Child Development Training Program, Iowa State University.

Miller, K. (1985). *Ages and stages.* Tellshare Publishing Co., 696 Plain St., Marshfield, MA 02050.

See references on pages 14–16, 32–33, and 61.

Adults know that 3-year-olds do not usually understand or remember the rules. Guidance reasons that are specific to a real situation and that are demonstrated repeatedly are more likely to impress young children.

PART 5

NAEYC Position Statement on Developmentally Appropriate Practice in Programs for 4- and 5-Year-Olds

Background information

In the mid 1980s, a great deal of public attention has focused on the quality of our nation's educational system. Early childhood education programs for 4- and 5-year-old children have become the focus of some controversy. Various issues are under debate, including the length of program day for this age group, the effect of various forms of sponsorship, and the nature of the curriculum.

Curriculum issues are of particular concern to early childhood educators in light of the increasingly widespread demand for use of inappropriate formal teaching techniques for young children, over-emphasis on achievement of narrowly defined academic skills, and increased reliance on psychometric tests to determine enrollment and retention in programs.

These trends are primarily the result of misconceptions about how young children learn (Elkind, 1986). In many cases, concerned adults, who want children to succeed, apply adult education standards to the curriculum for young children and pressure early childhood programs to demonstrate that children are "really learning." Many programs respond by emphasizing academic skill development with paper-and-pencil activities that are developmentally inappropriate for young children.

The National Association for the Education of Young Children (NAEYC), the nation's largest professional association of early childhood educators, believes that high quality, developmentally appropriate programs should be available for all 4- and 5-year-old children. NAEYC believes that quality is not determined by the length of the program day or by the sponsorship, although these factors can affect quality. NAEYC believes that a major determinant of the quality of an early childhood program is the degree to which the program is developmentally appropriate. This position statement describes both appropriate practices and inappropriate practices in early childhood programs. These beliefs about appropriate practice are supported by a growing body of both laboratory and clinical classroom research and theory. This statement is intended for use by teachers, parents, school administrators, policy makers, and others who provide educational programs for 4- and 5-year-olds.

Position Statement

How young children learn

Young children learn by doing. The work of Piaget (1950, 1972), Montessori (1964), Erikson (1950), and other child development theorists and researchers (Elkind, 1986; Kamii, 1985) has demonstrated that learning is a complex process that results from the interaction of children's own thinking and their experiences in the external world. Maturation is an important contributor to learning because it provides a framework from which children's learning proceeds. As children get older, they acquire new skills and experiences that facilitate the learning process. For example, as children grow physically, they are more able to manipulate and explore their own environment. Also, as children mature, they are more able to understand the point of view of other people.

Knowledge is not something that is given to children as though they were empty vessels to be filled. Children acquire knowledge about the physical and social worlds in which they live through playful interaction with objects and people. Children do not need to be forced to learn; they are motivated by their own desire to make sense of their world.

How to teach young children

How young children learn should determine how teachers of young children teach. The word *teach* tends to imply *telling* or *giving information*. But the correct way to teach young children is not to lecture or verbally instruct them. Teachers of young children are more like guides or facilitators (Forman & Kuschner, 1983; Lay-Dopyera & Dopyera, 1986; Piaget, 1972). They prepare the environment so that it provides stimulating, challenging materials and activities for children. Then, teachers closely observe to see what children understand and pose additional challenges to push their thinking further.

For children to fully understand and remember what they have learned, whether it is related to reading, mathematics, or other subject matter areas, the information must be meaningful to the child in context of the child's experience and development.

Children work individually or in small, informal groups most of the time.

Interactions and activities are designed to develop children's self-esteem and positive feelings toward learning.

Subjects & Predicates

Developmentally appropriate practice for 4- and 5-year-olds

Developmentally appropriate teaching strategies are based on knowledge of how young children learn. Curriculum derives from many sources such as the knowledge base of various disciplines, society, culture, and parents' desires. The degree to which both teaching strategies and the curriculum are developmentally appropriate is a major determinant of program quality. Developmentally appropriate programs are both age appropriate and individually appropriate; that is, the program is designed for the age group served and implemented with attention to the needs and differences of the individual children enrolled.

Because people develop concepts from both positive and negative examples, the components of a program for 4- and 5-year-olds are described here both in terms of what is appropriate and what is *not* appropriate practice. These components overlap considerably and have been identified here for purposes of clarity only.

Outdoor activity is planned daily so children can develop large muscle skills, learn about outdoor environments, and express themselves freely and loudly.

Marietta Lynch

It is possible to drill children until they can correctly recite pieces of information such as the alphabet or the numbers from 1 to 20. However, children's responses to rote tasks do not reflect real understanding of the information. For children to understand fully and remember what they have learned, whether it is related to reading, mathematics, or other subject matter areas, the information must be meaningful to the child in context of the child's experience and development.

Learning information in meaningful context is not only essential for children's understanding and development of concepts, but is also important for stimulating motivation in children. If learning is relevant for children, they are more likely to persist with a task and to be motivated to learn more.

53

Integrated Components of
APPROPRIATE and INAPPROPRIATE Practice for
4- AND 5-YEAR-OLD CHILDREN

Component	APPROPRIATE Practice	INAPPROPRIATE Practice
Curriculum goals	• Experiences are provided that meet children's needs and stimulate learning in all developmental areas—physical, social, emotional, and intellectual.	• Experiences are narrowly focused on the child's intellectual development without recognition that all areas of a child's development are interrelated.
	• Each child is viewed as a unique person with an individual pattern and timing of growth and development. The curriculum and adults' interaction are responsive to individual differences in ability and interests. Different levels of ability, development, and learning styles are expected, accepted, and used to design appropriate activities.	• Children are evaluated only against a predetermined measure, such as a standardized group norm or adult standard of behavior. All are expected to perform the same tasks and achieve the same narrowly defined, easily measured skills.
	• Interactions and activities are designed to develop children's self-esteem and positive feelings toward learning.	• Children's worth is measured by how well they conform to rigid expectations and perform on standardized tests.
Teaching strategies	• Teachers prepare the environment for children to learn through active exploration and interaction with adults, other children, and materials.	• Teachers use highly structured, teacher-directed lessons almost exclusively.
	• Children select many of their own activities from among a variety of learning areas the teacher prepares, including dramatic play, blocks, science, math, games and puzzles, books, recordings, art, and music.	• The teacher directs all the activity, deciding what children will do and when. The teacher does most of the activity for the children, such as cutting shapes, performing steps in an experiment.
	• Children are expected to be physically and mentally active. Children choose from among activities the teacher has set up or the children spontaneously initiate.	• Children are expected to sit down, watch, be quiet, and listen, or do paper-and-pencil tasks for inappropriately long periods of time. A major portion of time is spent passively sitting, listening, and waiting.
	• Children work individually or in small, informal groups most of the time.	• Large group, teacher-directed instruction is used most of the time.
	• Children are provided concrete learning activities with materials and people relevant to their own life experiences.	• Workbooks, ditto sheets, flashcards, and other similarly structured abstract materials dominate the curriculum.

Component	APPROPRIATE Practice	INAPPROPRIATE Practice
Teaching strategies (*continued*)	• Teachers move among groups and individuals to facilitate children's involvement with materials and activities by asking questions, offering suggestions, or adding more complex materials or ideas to a situation.	• Teachers dominate the environment by talking to the whole group most of the time and telling children what to do.
	• Teachers accept that there is often more than one right answer. Teachers recognize that children learn from self-directed problem solving and experimentation.	• Children are expected to respond correctly with one right answer. Rote memorization and drill are emphasized.
Guidance of social-emotional development	• Teachers facilitate the development of self-control in children by using positive guidance techniques such as modeling and encouraging expected behavior, redirecting children to a more acceptable activity, and setting clear limits. Teachers' expectations match and respect children's developing capabilities.	• Teachers spend a great deal of time enforcing rules, punishing unacceptable behavior, demeaning children who misbehave, making children sit and be quiet, or refereeing disagreements.
	• Children are provided many opportunities to develop social skills such as cooperating, helping, negotiating, and talking with the person involved to solve interpersonal problems. Teachers facilitate the development of these positive social skills at all times.	• Children work individually at desks or tables most of the time or listen to teacher directions in the total group. Teachers intervene to resolve disputes or enforce classroom rules and schedules.
Language development and literacy	• Children are provided many opportunities to see how reading and writing are useful before they are instructed in letter names, sounds, and word identification. Basic skills develop when they are meaningful to children. An abundance of these types of activities is provided to develop language and literacy through meaningful experience: listening to and reading stories and poems; taking field trips; dictating stories; seeing classroom charts and other print in use; participating in dramatic play and other experiences requiring communication; talking informally with other children and adults; and experimenting with writing by drawing, copying, and inventing their own spelling.	• Reading and writing instruction stresses isolated skill development such as recognizing single letters, reciting the alphabet, singing the alphabet song, coloring within predefined lines, or being instructed in correct formation of letters on a printed line.

Component	APPROPRIATE Practice	INAPPROPRIATE Practice
Cognitive development	Children develop understanding of concepts about themselves, others, and the world around them through observation, interacting with people and real objects, and seeking solutions to concrete problems. Learnings about math, science, social studies, health, and other content areas are all integrated through meaningful activities such as those when children build with blocks; measure sand, water, or ingredients for cooking; observe changes in the environment; work with wood and tools; sort objects for a purpose; explore animals, plants, water, wheels and gears; sing and listen to music from various cultures; and draw, paint, and work with clay. Routines are followed that help children keep themselves healthy and safe.	Instruction stresses isolated skill development through memorization and rote, such as counting, circling an item on a worksheet, memorizing facts, watching demonstrations, drilling with flashcards, or looking at maps. Children's cognitive development is seen as fragmented in content areas such as math, science, or social studies, and times are set aside to concentrate on each area.
Physical development	Children have daily opportunities to use large muscles, including running, jumping, and balancing. Outdoor activity is planned daily so children can develop large muscle skills, learn about outdoor environments, and express themselves freely and loudly.	Opportunity for large muscle activity is limited. Outdoor time is limited because it is viewed as interfering with instructional time or, if provided, is viewed as recess (a way to get children to use up excess energy), rather than an integral part of children's learning environment.
	Children have daily opportunities to develop small muscles skills through play activities such as pegboards, puzzles, painting, cutting, and other similar activities.	Small motor activity is limited to writing with pencils, or coloring predrawn forms, or similar structured lessons.
Aesthetic development	Children have daily opportunities for aesthetic expression and appreciation through art and music. Children experiment and enjoy various forms of music. A variety of art media are available for creative expression, such as easel and finger painting and clay.	Art and music are provided only when time permits. Art consists of coloring predrawn forms, copying an adult-made model of a product, or following other adult-prescribed directions.
Motivation	Children's natural curiosity and desire to make sense of their world are used to motivate them to become involved in learning activities.	Children are required to participate in all activities to obtain the teacher's approval, to obtain extrinsic rewards like stickers or privileges, or to avoid punishment.

Component	APPROPRIATE Practice	INAPPROPRIATE Practice
Parent-teacher relations	• Teachers work in partnership with parents, communicating regularly to build mutual understanding and greater consistency for children.	• Teachers communicate with parents only about problems or conflicts. Parents view teachers as experts and feel isolated from their child's experiences.
Assessment of children	• Decisions that have a major impact on children (such as enrollment, retention, assignment to remedial classes) are based primarily on information obtained from observations by teachers and parents, not on the basis of a single test score. Developmental assessment of children's progress and achievement is used to plan curriculum, identify children with special needs, communicate with parents, and evaluate the program's effectiveness.	• Psychometric tests are used as the sole criterion to prohibit entrance to the program or to recommend that children be retained or placed in remedial classrooms.
Program entry	• In public schools, there is a place for every child of legal entry age, regardless of the developmental level of the child. No public school program should deny access to children on the basis of results of screening or other arbitrary determinations of the child's lack of readiness. The educational system adjusts to the developmental needs and levels of the children it serves; children are not expected to adapt to an inappropriate system.	• Eligible-age children are denied entry to kindergarten or retained in kindergarten because they are judged not ready on the basis of inappropriate and inflexible expectations.
Teacher qualifications	• Teachers are qualified to work with 4- and 5-year-olds through college-level preparation in Early Childhood Education or Child Development and supervised experience with this age group.	• Teachers with no specialized training or supervised experience working with 4- and 5-year-olds are viewed as qualified because they are state certified, regardless of the level of certification.
Staffing	• The group size and ratio of teachers to children is limited to enable individualized and age-appropriate programming. Four- and 5-year-olds are in groups of no more than 20 children with 2 adults.	• Because older children can function reasonably well in large groups, it is assumed that group size and number of adults can be the same for 4- and 5-year-olds as for elementary grades.

Bibliography

These references include both laboratory and clinical classroom research to document the broad-based literature that forms the foundation for sound practice in early childhood education.

Related position statements

International Reading Association. (1985). *Literacy and pre-first grade.* Newark, DE: International Reading Association.

NAEYC. (1984). *Accreditation criteria and procedures of the National Academy of Early Childhood Programs.* Washington, DC: NAEYC.

NAEYC. (1986). *Position statement on developmentally appropriate practice in early childhood programs serving children from birth through age 8.*

Nebraska State Board of Education. (1984). *Position statement on kindergarten.* Lincoln, NE: Nebraska State Department of Education.

Southern Association on Children Under Six. (1984, July). A statement on developmentally appropriate educational experiences for kindergarten. *Dimensions, 12*(4), 25.

Southern Association on Children Under Six. (1986). *Position statement on quality four-year-old programs in public schools. Dimensions, 14*(3), 29.

Southern Association on Children Under Six. (1986). *Position statement on quality child care. Dimensions, 14*(4), p. 28.

State Department of Education, Columbia, South Carolina. (1983, rev. ed.). *Early childhood education in South Carolina. Learning experiences for 3-, 4-, and 5-year-old children.*

Texas Association for the Education of Young Children. (no date). *Developmentally appropriate kindergarten reading programs: A position statement.*

Developmentally appropriate practices and curriculum goals

Biber, B. (1984). *Early education and psycological development.* New Haven: Yale University Press.

Council of Chief State School Officers. (1988). *Early chilhood and family education: Foundations for success.* Washington, DC: Author.

Elkind, D. (1986, May). Formal education and early childhood education: An essential difference. *Phi Delta Kappan,* 631–636.

Elkind, D. (1988). Early childhood education on its own terms. In S. L. Kagan & E. Zigler (Eds.), *Handbook of research in early childhood education* (pp. 185–211). New York: Free Press.

Elkind, D. (1988). The resistance to developmentally appropriate educational practice with young children: The real issue. In C. Warger (Ed.), *Public school early childhood programs.* Alexandria, VA: Association for Supervision and Curriculum Development.

Erikson, E. (1950). *Childhood and society.* New York: Norton.

Kagan, S. L. (Ed.), (1989). Early care and education: Reflecting on options and opportunities [special issue]. *Phi Delta Kappan, 71* (2).

Katz, L., Evangelou, D., & Hartman, J. A. (in press). *The case for mixed-age grouping.* Washington, DC: NAEYC.

Kohlberg, L., & Mayer, R. (1972). Development as the arm of education. *Harvard Educational Review, 42,* 449–496.

Marx, F., & Seligson, M. (1988). *The public school early childhood study: The state survey.* New York: Bank Street College.

Missouri Department of Elementary and Secondary Education. (1989). *Project construct: Curriculum and assessment specifications.* St. Louis: Author.

Montessori, M. (1964). *The Montessori method.* Cambridge, MA: Robert Bentley.

National Association of State Boards of Education. (1988). *Right from the start: The report of the NASBE task force on early childhood education.* Alexandria, VA: Author.

Piaget, J. (1950). *The psychology of intelligence.* London: Routledge & Kegan Paul.

Piaget, J. (1952). *The origins of intelligence in children.* (M. Cook, Trans.) New York: Norton. (Original work published 1936).

Spodek, B. (1985). *Teaching in the early years* (3rd ed.). Englewood Cliffs, NJ: Prentice-Hall.

Weber, E. (1984). *Ideas influencing early childhood education: A theoretical analysis.* New York: Teachers College Press, Columbia University.

Teaching strategies

Fein, G. (1979). Play and the acquisition of symbols. In L. Katz (Ed.), *Current topics in early childhood education, Vol. 2.* Norwood, NJ: Ablex.

Fein, G., & Rivkin, M. (Eds.). (1986). *The young child at play: Reviews of research* (Vol. 4). Washington, DC: NAEYC.

Fromberg, D. (1986). Play. In C. Seefeldt (Ed.), *Early childhood curriculum: A review of current research.* New York: Teachers College Press, Columbia University.

Forman, G., & Kuschner, D. (1983). *The child's construction of knowledge: Piaget for teaching children.* Washington, DC: NAEYC.

Herron, R., & Sutton-Smith, B. (1974). *Child's play.* New York: Wiley.

Kamii, C. (1985). Leading primary education toward excellence: Beyond worksheets and drill. *Young Children, 40*(6), 3–9.

Languis, M., Sanders, T., & Tipps, S. (1980). *Brain and learning: Directions in early childhood education.* Washington, DC: NAEYC.

Lay-Dopyera, M., & Dopyera, J. (1986). Strategies for teaching. In C. Seefeldt (Ed.), *Early childhood curriculum: A review of current research.* New York: Teachers College Press, Columbia University.

Piaget, J. (1972). *Science of education and the psychology of the child* (rev. ed.). New York: Viking. (Original work published 1965)

Souweine, J. K., Crimmins, S., & Mazel, C. (1981). *Mainstreaming: Ideas for teaching young children.* Washington, DC: NAEYC.

Sponseller, D. (1982). Play and early education. In B. Spodek (Ed.), *Handbook of research in early childhood education.* New York: Free Press.

Guidance of socioemotional development

Asher, S. R., Renshaw, P. D., & Hymel, S. (1982). Peer relations and the development of social skills. In S. G. Moore & C. R. Cooper (Eds.), *The young child: Reviews of research* (Vol. 3, pp. 137–158). Washington, DC: NAEYC.

Erikson, E. (1950). *Childhood and society.* New York: Norton.

Greenberg, P. (in press). *Encouraging self-esteem and self-discipline: Character development infancy through age 8.* Washington, DC: NAEYC.

Honig, A. S. (1985). Research in review. Compliance, control, and discipline (Parts 1 & 2). *Young children, 40*(2), 50–58; *40*(3), 47–52.

Moore, S. (1982). Prosocial behavior in the early years: Parent and peer influences. In B. Spodek (Ed.), *Handbook of research in early childhood education.* New York: Free Press.

Read, K. H., Gardner, P., & Mahler, B. (1986). *Early childhood programs: A laboratory for human relationships* (8th ed.). New York: Holt, Rinehart & Winston.

Rubin, K., & Everett, B. (1982). Social perspective-taking in young children. In S. G. Moore & C. R. Cooper (Eds.), *The young child: Reviews of research* (Vol. 3, pp. 97–114). Washington, DC: NAEYC.

Stone, J. (1978). *A guide to discipline* (rev. ed.). Washington, DC: NAEYC.

Language development and literacy

Cazden, C. (Ed.). (1981). *Language in early childhood education* (rev. ed.). Washington, DC: NAEYC.

Ferreiro, E., & Teberosky, A. (1982). *Literacy before schooling.* Exeter, NH: Heinemann.

Genishi, C. (1986). Acquiring language and communicative competence. In C. Seefeldt (Ed.), *Early childhood curriculum: A review of current research.* New York: Teachers College Press, Columbia University.

Heibert, E. H. (1988). The role of literacy experiences in early childhood programs. *The Elementary School Journal, 89*(2), 161–172.

Lloyd-Jones, R., & Lunsford, A. A. (Eds.). (1988). *The English Coalition Conference: Democracy through language.* Urbana, IL: National Council of Teachers of English.

Schachter, F. F., & Strage, A. A. (1982). Adults' talk and children's language development. In S. G. Moore & C. R. Cooper (Eds.), *The young child: Reviews of research* (Vol. 3, pp. 79–96). Washington, DC: NAEYC.

Schickedanz, J. (1986). *More than the ABCs: The early stages of reading and writing.* Washington, DC: NAEYC.

Smith, F. (1982). *Understanding reading.* New York: Holt, Rinehart & Winston.

Strickland, D. S., & Morrow, L. M. (Eds.). (1988). *Emerging literacy: Young children learn to read and write.* Newark, DE: International Reading Association.

Willert, M., & Kamii, C. (1985). Reading in kindergarten: Direct versus indirect teaching. *Young Children, 40*(4), 3–9.

Cognitive development

DeVries, R., with Kohlberg, L. (1987). *Programs of early education: The constructivist view.* New York: Longman.

Forman, G., & Kaden, M. (1986). Research on science education in young children. In C. Seefeldt (Ed.), *Early childhood curriculum: A review of current research.* New York: Teachers College Press, Columbia University.

Goffin, S., & Tull, C. (1985). Problem solving: Encouraging active learning. *Young Children, 40*(3). 28–32.

Kamii, C. (1982). *Number in preschool and kindergarten.* Washington, DC: NAEYC.

Hawkins, D. (1970). Messing about in science. *ESS Reader.* Newton, MA: Education Development Center.

Hirsch, E. (Ed.). (1984). *The block book.* Washington, DC: NAEYC.

Holt, B. (1979). *Science with young children.* Washington, DC: NAEYC.

Sackoff, E., & Hart, R. (1984, Summer). Toys: Research and applications. *Children's Environments Quarterly, 1–2.*

Wellman, H. M. (1982). The foundations of knowledge: Concept development in the young child. In S. G. Moore & C. R. Cooper (Eds.), *The young child: Reviews of research* (Vol. 3, pp. 115–134). Washington, DC: NAEYC.

Physical development

Cratty, B. (1982). Motor development in early childhood: Critical issues for researchers in the 1980's. In B. Spodek (Ed.), *Handbook of research in early childhood education.* New York: Free Press.

Curtis, S. (1986). New views on movement development and implications for curriculum in early childhood education. In C. Seefeldt (Ed.). *Early childhood curriculum: A review of current research.* New York: Teachers College Press, Columbia University.

Aesthetic development

Davidson, L. (1985). Preschool children's tonal knowledge: Antecedents of scale. In J. Boswell (Ed.), *The young child and music: Contemporary principles in child development and music education. Proceedings of the Music in Early Childhood Conference* (pp. 25–40). Reston, VA: Music Educators National Conference.

Evans, E. D. (1984). Children's aesthetics. In L. G. Katz (Ed.), *Current topics in early childhood education* (Vol. 5, pp. 73–104). Norwood, NJ: Ablex.

Gilbert, J. P. (1981). Motoric music skill development in young children: A longitudinal investigation. *Psychology of Music, 9*(1), 21–24.

Greenberg, M. (1976). Music in early childhood education: A survey with recommendations. *Council for Research in Music Education, 45,* 1–20.

Lasky, L., & Mukerji, R. (1980). *Art: Basic for young children.* Washington, DC: NAEYC.

McDonald, D. T. (1979). *Music in our lives: The early years.* Washington, DC: NAEYC.

Seefeldt, C. (1986). The visual arts. In C. Seefeldt (Ed.), *The early childhood curriculum: A review of current research.* New York: Teachers College Press, Columbia University.

Smith, N. (1983). *Experience and art: Teaching children to paint.* New York: Teachers College Press, Columbia University.

Motivation

Elkind, D. (1986). Formal education and early childhood education: An essential difference. *Phi Delta Kappan,* 631–636.

Gottfried, A. (1983). Intrinsic motivation in young children. *Young Children, 39*(1), 64–73.

Parent-teacher relations

Croft, D. J. (1979). *Parents and teachers: A resource book for home, school, and community relations.* Belmont, CA: Wadsworth.

Gazda, G. M. (1973). *Human relations development: A manual for educators.* Boston: Allyn & Bacon.

Greenberg, P. (1989). Parents as partners in young children's development and education: A new American fad? Why does it matter? *Young Children, 44*(4), 61–74.

Honig, A. (1982). Parent involvement in early childhood education. In B. Spodek (Ed.), *Handbook of research in early childhood education.* New York: Free Press.

Katz, L. (1980). Mothering and teaching: Some significant distinctions. In L. Katz (Ed.), *Current topics in early childhood education* (Vol. 3, pp. 47–64). Norwood, NJ: Ablex.

Lightfoot, S. (1978). *Worlds apart: Relationships between families and schools.* New York: Basic.

Assessment of children

Cohen, D. H., Stern, V., & Balaban, N. (1983). *Observing and recording the behavior of young children* (3rd ed.). New York: Teachers College Press, Columbia University.

Goodwin, W., & Goodwin, L. (1982). Measuring young children. In B. Spodek (Ed.), *Handbook of research in early childhood education.* New York: Free Press.

Meisels, S. (1985). *Developmental screening in early childhood.* Washington, DC: NAEYC.

Standards for educational and psychological testing. (1985). Washington, DC: American Psychological Association, American Educational Research Association, and National Council on Measurement in Education.

Teacher qualifications and staffing

Almy, M. (1982). Day care and early childhood education. In E. Zigler & E. Gordon (Eds.), *Daycare: Scientific and social policy issues* (pp. 476–495). Boston: Auburn House.

Feeney, S., & Chun, R. (1985). Research in review. Effective teachers of young children. *Young Children, 41*(1), 47–52.

NAEYC. (1982). *Early childhood teacher education guidelines for four- and five-year programs.* Washington, DC: NAEYC.

Ruopp, R., Travers, J., Glantz, F., & Coelen, C. (1979). *Children at the center. Final report of the National Day Care Study, Vol. 1.* Cambridge, MA: Abt Associates.

PART 6
Transitions: Changes and Challenges

A toddler enters child care for the first time.

A 3-year-old moves from the toddler group to the preschool group in a child care center.

A Head Start graduate enters kindergarten.

At 3:00 each day, a first grader moves from the classroom to the after-school child care group.

All change is stressful. But for young children who have limited experience and few well-developed coping strategies, change can be very stressful. When children move from one program to another or from one group to another within a program, adjustments are always necessary. However, the amount of stress and the time required to make successful adjustments can be lessened significantly if teachers and administrators plan and work together to implement smooth transitions.

Following are four key elements to consider to help ensure successful transitions for young children and their families (Glicksman & Hills, 1981; U.S. Department of Health and Human Services, 1987):

1. **Ensure program continuity by providing developmentally appropriate curriculum for all age levels in all educational settings.**

The more variance that exists in developmental expectations and teaching practices between different settings or groups, the more stressful the transition will be for young children. When the kindergarten program is more like a second grade with desks and papers than like a preschool with blocks and dramatic play props, the change is so abrupt that many children have difficulty adapting. Unfortunately, when such disparity arises, the preschool teacher too often introduces inappropriate academic instruction to help her group of children "get ready" for kindergarten. In such a situation, modifying an appropriate preschool program is a misguided attempt to ease the child's transition. The cause of the problem is not the preschool but the kindergarten—its curriculum is the area in need of attention.

Differences in program content, teaching strategies, and expectations of children are not only to be expected, they are desirable. Programs *should* vary depending on the age of children and the needs and interests of individual children and families. Nevertheless, the more developmentally appropriate different programs are, the smoother and more successful children's transitions will be between different programs or groups.

2. **Maintain ongoing communication and cooperation between staff at different programs.**

Children's transitions can be facilitated if teachers in one setting such as a preschool or child care center work together with teachers in settings where children will go, such as a public school kingergarten. Visits to

It is stressful for young children to move from home to school, from one program to another, from child care to school, or from one grade to another within *the school. The amount of stress and the time required to adjust successfully can be significantly lessened if parents, teachers, and administrators focus together on easing the difficulty.*

Subjects & Predicates

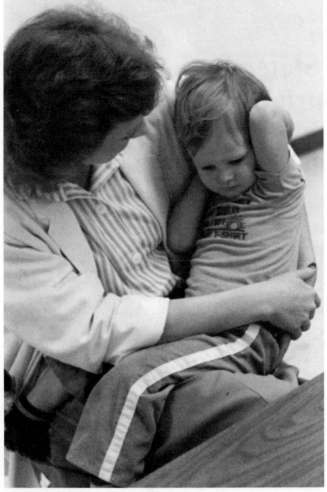

Nancy P. Alexander

We need to be sure that our comments about what's coming next do not sound like threats: "You better learn to behave— in kindergarten the teacher will expect you to know what to do." Remarks like this frighten children.

3. Prepare children for the transition.

"Next year you'll be in kindergarten and then you won't be allowed to do that!"

"You'd better study this now because you have to know it when you start third grade."

"At the center, you'll have to use the potty like a big boy."

Unfortunately messages like the above may be the only preparation children get for a major life change. Vague warnings about unfamiliar situations only serve to heighten children's anxieties about change. A more appropriate approach is to give children firsthand experiences, preferably by visiting the new classroom or building and meeting the teacher. If such direct contact is impossible, a letter or phone call from the new teacher or caregiver can be almost as effective. Children need time to talk about their feelings and sensitive adults to listen and help prepare them for the exciting and positive changes that are a natural part of growing up.

4. Involve parents in the transitions.

Parents usually feel as anxious as their children about child care and school transitions and children sense their stress. If parents' tensions are soothed, children will also face the change more calmly and confidently. Communication is the key to effective involvement of families. Transitions are more successful when teachers inform parents of expectations and also listen to parents' concerns and goals for their children.

Attention to these four critical elements will lessen the negative impact of transition. Too often today, children's lives are unnecessarily fragmented. Transitions that formerly occurred once a year now occur several times daily. Parents and teachers need to work together to minimize the number of transitions required of children and to ease the transitions that are a necessary and healthy by-product of development.

References

Glicksman, K., & Hills, T. (1981). *Easing the child's transition between home, child care center and school: A guide for early childhood educators.* Trenton: New Jersey Department of Education.

U.S. Department of Health and Human Services, Administration for Children, Youth and Families. (1987). *Easing the transition from preschool to kindergarten.* Washington, DC: Author.

programs can be arranged for children and parents. Teachers can visit each other's program to note similarities and differences for which to prepare children. Such cooperation is advantageous for the teacher whose classroom or program the child will attend because the child is better prepared and less fearful. The teacher who is left behind also benefits by broadening professional contacts and knowing that she has fulfilled her professional responsibility to meet the developmental needs of the children in her care.

PART 7

NAEYC Position Statement on Developmentally Appropriate Practice in the Primary Grades Serving 5- Through 8-Year-Olds

The current trend toward critical examination of our nation's educational system has recently included concerns about the quality of education provided in elementary schools (Bennett, 1986; Office of Educational Research and Improvement, 1986). Concerns have been raised because, in response to calls for "back to basics" and improved standardized test scores, many elementary schools have narrowed the curriculum and adopted instructional approaches that are incompatible with current knowledge about how young children learn and develop. Specifically, rote learning of academic skills is often emphasized rather than active, experiential learning in a meaningful context. As a result, many children are being taught academic skills but are not learning to apply those skills in context and are not developing more complex thinking skills like conceptualizing and problem solving (Bennett, 1986).

The National Asociation for the Education of Young Children (NAEYC), the nation's largest organization of early childhood educators, defines early childhood as the years from birth through age 8. NAEYC believes that on index of the quality of primary education is the extent to which the curruculum and instructional methods are developmentally appropriate for children 5 through 8 years of age. The purpose of this position statement is to describe both developmentally appropriate and inappropriate practices in the primary grades. This position statement relfects the most current knowledge of teaching and learning as derived from theory, research, and practice. This statement is intended for use by teachers, parents, school administrators, policymakers, and others who make decisions about primary grade educational programs. (NAEYC's Position Statement on Developmentally Appropriate Practice in Programs for 4- and 5-Year-Olds specifically defines appropriate practices for prekindergarten and kindergarten programs; see pp. 51–59.)

Background information

Classrooms serving primary-age children are typically part of larger institutions and complex educational systems with many levels of administration and supervision. Classroom teachers may have little control over the curriculum or policies they implement. However, ensuring developmentally appropriate practice in primary education requires the efforts of the entire group of educators who are responsible for planning and implementing curriculum—teachers, curriculum supervisors, principals, and superintendents. At the same time, ensuring developmentally appropriate practice is the professional obligation of each individual educator. No professional should abdicate this responsibility in the absence of mutual understanding and support of colleagues or supervisors. This position statement is intended to support the current appropriate practices of many primary-grade programs and to help guide the decisions of administrators so that developmentally appropriate practices for primary-age children become more widely accepted, supported, and followed.

Curriculum derives from several sources: the child, the content, and the society. The curriculum in early childhood programs is typically a balance of child-centered and content-centered curriculum. For example, good preschools present rich content in a curriculum that is almost entirely child-centered. As children progress into the primary grades, the emphasis on content gradually expands as determined by the school, the local community, and the society. The challenge for curriculum planners and teachers is to ensure that the content of the curriculum is taught so as to take optimum advantage of the child's natural abilities, interests, and enthusiasm for learning.

Development and learning in primary-age children

Integrated development and learning

In order to provide developmentally appropriate primary education, it is essential to understand the development that typically occurs during this period of life and to understand how 5- through 8-year-old children learn. We can then derive principles of appropriate practice for primary-age children. One of the most important premises of human development is that all domains of development—physical, social, emotional, and cognitive—are integrated. Development in one dimension influences and is influenced by development in other dimensions. This premise is violated when schools place a great emphasis on the cognitive domain while minimizing other aspects of children's development. Because development cannot be neatly separated into parts, failure to attend to all aspects of an individual child's development is often the root cause of a child's failure in school. For example, when a child lacks social skills and is neglected or rejected by peers, her or his ability to work cooperatively in a school setting is impaired. As interest lags, the child's learning may also be impaired, and she or he may become truant or eventually drop out (Burton, 1987). *The relevant principle of instruction is that teachers of young children must always be cognizant of "the whole child."*

Children's learning, like development, is integrated during the early years. One of the major pressures on elementary teachers has always been the need to "cover the curriculum." Frequently, they have tried to do so by tightly scheduling discrete time segments for each subject. This approach ignores the fact that young children do not need to distinguish learning by subject area. For example, they extend their knowledge of reading and writing when they work on social studies projects; they learn mathematical concepts through music and physical education (Van Deusen-Henkel & Argondizza, 1987). *The relevant principle of instruction is that throughout the primary grades the curriculum should be integrated* (Katz & Chard, in press).

Integration of curriculum is accomplished in several ways. The curriculum may be planned around themes that are selected by the children or by the teacher based on the children's interests. For example, children may be interested in the ocean because they live near it. Children may work on projects related to the ocean during which they do reading, writing, math, science, social studies, art, and music. Such projects involve sustained, cooperative effort and involvement over several days and perhaps weeks.

Integrated curriculum may also be facilitated by providing learning areas in which children plan and select their activities. For example, the classroom may include "a fully-equipped publishing center, complete with materials for writing, illustrating, typing, and binding student-made books; a science area with animals and plants for observation, and books to study; and other similar areas" (Van Deusen-Henkel & Argon-

dizza, 1987). In such a classroom, children learn reading as they discover information about science; they learn writing as they work together on interesting projects. Such classrooms also provide opportunities for spontaneous play, recognizing that primary-age children continue to learn in all areas through unstructured play—either alone or with other children.

Physical development

During the primary years, children's physical growth tends to slow down as compared to the extremely rapid physical growth that occurred during the first 5 years of life. Children gain greater control over their bodies and are able to sit and attend for longer periods of time. However, primary-age children are far from mature physically and need to be active. Primary-grade children are more fatigued by long periods of sitting than by running, jumping, or bicycling. Physical action is essential for these children to refine their developing skills, like batting a ball, skipping rope, or balancing on a beam. Expressing their newly acquired physical power and control also enhances their self-esteem.

Physical activity is vital for children's cognitive growth as well. When presented with an abstract concept, children need physical actions to help them grasp the concept in much the same way that adults need vivid examples and illustrations to grasp unfamiliar concepts. But unlike adults, primary-age children are almost totally dependent on first-hand experiences. *Therefore, an important principle of practice for primary-age children is that they should be engaged in active, rather than passive, activities* (Katz & Chard, in press). For example, children should manipulate real objects and learn through hands-on, direct experiences rather than be expected to sit and listen for extended periods of time.

Cognitive development

The learning patterns of primary-age children are greatly affected by the gradual shift from preoperational to concrete operational thought, a major dimension of cognitive development during these years (Piaget, 1952; Piaget & Inhelder, 1969). Between 6 and 9 years of age, children begin to acquire the mental ability to think about and solve problems in their heads because they can then manipulate objects symbolically—no longer always having to touch or move them. This is a major cognitive achievement for children that extends their ability to solve problems. Despite this change in approach to cognitive tasks, however, primary-age children are still not capable of thinking and problem solving in the same way as adults. While they can symbolically or mentally manipulate objects, it will be some time before they can mentally manipu-

Elaine M. Ward

Provide opportunities for 5- to 8-year-olds to do real things and to write, read, and play in relation to the learning activity.

late symbols to, for example, solve mathematical problems such as missing addends or to grasp algebra. For this reason, primary-age children still need real things to think about. Accordingly, while children can use symbols such as words and numbers to represent objects and relations, they still need concrete reference points. *Therefore, a principle of practice for primary-age children is that the curriculum provide many developmentally appropriate materials for children to explore and think about and opportunities for interaction and communication with other children and adults. Similarly, the content of the curriculum must be relevant, engaging, and meaningful to the children themselves* (Katz & Chard, in press).

Young children construct their own knowledge from experience. In schools employing appropriate practices, young children are provided with many challenging opportunities to use and develop the thinking skills they bring with them and to identify and solve problems that interest them. In addition, appropriate schools recognize that some thinking skills, such as understanding mathematical place value and "borrowing" in subtraction, are beyond the cognitive ca-

pacity of children who are developing concrete operational thinking and so do *not* introduce these skills to most children until they are 8 or 9 years of age (Kamii, 1985).

Children in the stage of concrete operations typically attain other skills that have important implications for schooling (Elkind, 1981). Among these is the ability to take another person's point of view, which vastly expands the child's communication skills. Primary-age children can engage in interactive conversations with adults as well with other children and can use the power of verbal communication, including joking and teasing. Research demonstrates that engaging in conversation strengthens children's abilities to communicate, express themselves, and reason (Nelson, 1985; Wells, 1983; Wilkinson, 1984). Research also indicates that adults can help prolong and expand children's conversations by making appropriate comments (Blank, 1985). *Therefore, relevant principles of practice are that primary-age children be provided opportunities to work in small groups on projects that "provide rich content for conversation" and that teachers facilitate discussion among children by making comments and soliciting children's opinions and ideas* (Katz & Chard, in press).

Social-emotional and moral development

Children of primary-grade age are becoming intensely interested in peers. Establishing productive, positive social and working relationships with other children close to their age provides the foundation for developing a sense of social competence. Recent research provides powerful evidence that children who fail to develop minimal social competence and are rejected or neglected by their peers are at significant risk to drop out of school, to become delinquent, and to experience mental health problems in adulthood (Asher, Hymel, & Renshaw, 1984; Asher, Renshaw, & Hymel, 1982; Cowen, Pederson, Babigian, Izzo, & Trost, 1973; Gronlund & Holmlund, 1985; Parker & Asher, 1986). Research also demonstrates that adult intervention and coaching can help children develop better peer relationships (Asher & Williams, 1987; Burton, 1987). *The relevant principle of practice is that teachers recognize the importance of developing positive peer group relationships and provide opportunities and support for cooperative small group projects that not only develop cognitive ability but promote peer interaction.*

The ability to work and relate effectively with peers is only one dimension of the major social-emotional developmental task of the early school years—the development of a sense of competence. Erikson (1963) describes this major developmental challenge as the child's struggle between developing a sense of industry or feelings of inferiority. *To develop this sense of industry or a sense of competence, primary-age children need to acquire the knowledge and skills recognized by our culture as important, foremost among which are the abilities to read and write and to calculate numerically.* If children do not succeed in acquiring the competence needed to function in the world, they develop a sense of inferiority or inadequacy that may seriously inhibit future performance. The urge to master the skills of esteemed adults and older children is as powerful as the urge to stand and walk is for 1-year-olds. Yet when expectations exceed children's capabilities and children are pressured to acquire skills too far beyond their ability, their motivation to learn as well as their self-esteem may be impaired. A major cause of negative self-image for children this age is failure to succeed in school, for instance failing to learn to read "on schedule" or being assigned to the lowest ability math group.

At about age 6, most children begin to internalize moral rules of behavior and thus acquire a conscience. Children's behavior often shows that they find it difficult to live with and by their new self-monitoring and that they need adults' assistance. *Teachers and parents need to help children accept their conscience and achieve self-control.* In appropriate classrooms, teachers use positive guidance techniques, such as modeling and logical consequences, to help children learn appropriate behavior, rather than punishing, criticizing, or comparing children. In addition, teachers involve children in establishing and enforcing the few, basic rules necessary for congenial group living. Sensitive teachers ask children what they think of their work or behavior. The teacher points out how pleased the child must feel when a goal is accomplished. If achievement is lacking, the teacher empathizes with a child's feelings and solicits her or his ideas as to how to improve the situation.

Children at this age also begin to make more accurate judgments about what is true and false and to rigidly apply their newfound understanding of rules (Elkind, 1981). Their newly formed consciences are often excessively strict. For example, they may treat every little mistake as a major crime, deserving of terrible punishment. Adults help children assess mistakes realistically and find ways of correcting them. Children's developing consciences especially insist on fairness and adherence to rules. They closely observe adult infractions so it is very helpful for adults to be fair and obey rules. Sensitive teachers appeal to children's respect for fairness and rules when it comes to their interactions with others or when it is necessary to deny their requests, for example, "If I allow you to do that, I would be unfair to the others and you couldn't

trust that, some other time, I wouldn't also be unfair to you" (Furman, 1980, 1987a, 1987b).

Despite their increased independence and developing consciences, 5-, 6-, 7-, and even 8-year-old children still need supervision and the support of trusted adults. As a result, children in this age group should not be expected to supervise themselves in school or after school for extended periods of time. Teachers and parents provide opportunities for children to develop independence and assume responsibility but should not expect primary-age children to display adult levels of self-control.

Individual differences and appropriate practices

Knowledge of age-appropriate expectations is one dimension of developmentally appropriate practice, but equally important is knowledge of what is individually appropriate for the specific children in a classroom. Although universal and predictable sequences of human development appear to exist, a major premise of developmentally appropriate practice is that each child is unique and has an individual pattern and timing of growth, as well as individual personality, learning style, and family background. Children's sense of self-worth derives in large part from their experiences within the family. When children enter school, their self-esteem comes to include the school's opinion of their family. When children sense that teachers respect and value their families, and respect the particular cultural patterns by which their family lives, their own sense of self-esteem and competence is enhanced. It is developmentally appropriate to view parents as integral partners in the educational process. Teachers should communicate frequently and respectfully with parents and welcome them into the classroom. Teachers need to recognize that cultural variety is the American norm and that children's abilities are most easily demonstrated through familiar cultural forms (Hilliard, 1986).

Enormous variance exists in the timing of individual development that is within the normal range. Developmentally appropriate schools are flexible in their expectations about when and how children will acquire certain competencies. Recognition of individual differences dictates that a variety of teaching methods be used (Durkin, 1980; Katz & Chard, in press). Because children's backgrounds, experiences, socialization, and learning styles are so different, any one method is likely to succeed with some children and fail with others. *The principle of practice is that the younger the children and the more diverse their backgrounds, the wider the variety of teaching methods and materials required* (Durkin, 1980; Katz & Chard, in press; Katz, Raths, & Torres, undated).

Developmentally appropriate schools are also flexible in how they group children. Rigid adherence to chronological age/grade groupings or ability groupings is inappropriate. For this reason, some schools provide ungraded primary or several alternatives such as 2- or 3-year combination classrooms of 5-, 6-, and 7-year-olds or 6-, 7-, and 8-year-olds. Some schools recognize that many 8-year-olds are developmentally more like 9- and 10-year-olds and others more like 6- or 7-year-olds. Such combination classrooms or ungraded primary schools provide a vehicle for preserving heterogeneous groups while also providing more time for children to develop at their own pace and acquire early literacy and mathematical skills.

Most children have individual, personal interests and needs just as adults do. Most children are motivated to learn by an intense desire to make sense out of their world and to achieve the competencies desired by the culture. Children are learning all the time although they may not be learning the prescribed curriculum presented by the teacher (Elkind, 1981). For example, some children learn quickly that they are not smart (in the eyes of their teacher) or that their ideas are unimportant; other children learn that they are not effective group members. The learning that takes place in the primary grades far exceeds the knowledge and skills designated in the written curriculum. Research (Covington, 1984; Stipek, 1984) shows that unless they have a physical disability or illness or have been abused, preschool and kindergarten children are optimistic about their own powers and arrive at school confident that they will achieve. They are developing and acquiring skills so rapidly that they naturally assume that what they cannot do today will be possible tomorrow (Hills, 1986). As children get older, they begin to understand the limits of their own abilities and they also become more aware of social comparison. In the normal course of development, children compare themselves to others favorably and unfavorably. This information becomes part of their self-concept and can affect their motivation for activity. For example, children learn whether they are better at science or art or baseball and such learning influences life decisions. *Unfortunately, when schools unduly rely on competition and comparison among children, they hasten the process of children's own social comparison, lessen children's optimism about their own abilities and school in general, and stifle motivation to learn* (Hills, 1986).

During the early years, children are not only learning knowledge and skills, they are acquiring dispositions toward learning and school that could last a lifetime (Elkind, 1987; Gottfried, 1983; Katz, 1985; Katz & Chard, in press). Dispositions are "relatively enduring habits of mind and action, or tendencies to respond to events or situations," for example, curiosity, humor, or helpfulness (Katz & Chard, in press). *Longitudinal research indicates that curriculum and teaching methods should be designed so that children not only acquire knowledge and skills, but they also acquire the disposition or inclination to use them.* Compelling evidence exists asserting that overemphasis on mastery of narrowly defined reading and arithmetic skills and excessive drill and practice of skills that have been mastered threaten children's dispositions to use the skills they have acquired (Dweck, 1986; Katz & Chard, in press; Schweinhart, Weikart, & Larner, 1986; Walberg, 1984). It is as important for children to acquire the desire to read during the primary grades as it is for them to acquire the mechanics of reading. Similarly, it is as important for children to want to apply math to solve problems as it is for them to know their math facts.

The primary grades hold the potential for starting children on a course of lifelong learning. Whether schools achieve this potential for children is largely dependent on the degree to which teachers adopt principles of developmentally appropriate practice. The principles of practice described here have historical roots that include Dewey's progressive education (Biber, Murphy, Woodcock, & Black, 1942; Dewey, 1899), and the open education movement of the 1960s (Barth, 1972; Weber, 1971). Although the principles are similar in many instances to principles espoused by both those movements, this position statement does not advocate a return to practices of the past but rather builds on previous experience and reflects the knowledge acquired in the interim. Theory and research regarding effective curriculum and instruction have increased enormously in recent years and have contributed to our greater understanding of the teaching/learning process. This position statement reflects the most current knowledge of teaching and learning as derived from theory, research, and practice.

The components of a primary grade educational program are described here both in terms of what is appropriate, or ideals to strive for, and what is inappropriate because people develop concepts from exposure to both positive and negative examples. While it is true that most elementary schools and classrooms exhibit some characteristics described here as inappropriate, many schools and classrooms incorporate elements of appropriate practice while many others are models of what is deemed professionally appropriate. (Integrated program components overlap considerably and are identified here separately for purposes of clarity only.)

INTEGRATED COMPONENTS OF
APPROPRIATE AND INAPPROPRIATE PRACTICE IN
THE PRIMARY GRADES

Component	APPROPRIATE Practice	INAPPROPRIATE Practice
Curriculum goals	• Curriculum is designed to develop children's knowledge and skills in all developmental areas—physical, social, emotional, and intellectual—and to help children learn how to learn—to establish a foundation for lifelong learning.	• Curriculum is narrowly focused on the intellectual domain with intellectual development narrowly defined as acquisition of discrete, technical academic skills, without recognition that all areas of children's development are interrelated.
	• Curriculum and instruction are designed to develop children's self-esteem, sense of competence, and positive feelings toward learning.	• Children's worth is measured by how well they conform to group expectations, such as their ability to read at grade level and their performance on standardized tests.
	• Each child is viewed as a unique person with an individual pattern and timing of growth. Curriculum and instruction are responsive to individual differences in ability and interests. Different levels of ability, development, and learning styles are expected, accepted, and used to design curriculum. Children are allowed to move at their own pace in acquiring important skills including those of writing, reading, spelling, math, social studies, science, art, music, health, and physical activity. For example, it is accepted that not every child will learn how to read at age 6; most will learn to read by 7; and some will need intensive exposure to appropriate literacy experiences to learn to read by age 8 or 9.	• Children are evaluated against a standardized group norm. All are expected to achieve the same narrowly defined, easily measured academic skills by the same predetermined time schedule typically determined by chronological age and grade level expectations.
Teaching strategies	• The curriculum is integrated so that children's learning in all traditional subject areas occurs primarily through projects and learning centers that teachers plan and that reflect children's interests and suggestions. Teachers guide children's involvement in projects and enrich the learning experience by extending children's ideas, responding to their questions, engaging them in conversation, and challenging their thinking.	• Curriculum is divided into separate subjects and time is carefully allotted for each with primary emphasis given each day to reading and secondary emphasis to math. Other subjects such as social studies, science, and health are covered if time permits. Art, music, and physical education are taught only once a week and only by teachers who are specialists in those areas.

Component	APPROPRIATE Practice	INAPPROPRIATE Practice
Teaching strategies *(continued)*	• The curriculum is integrated so that learning occurs primarily through projects, learning centers, and playful activities that reflect current interests of children. For example, a social studies project such as building and operating a store or a science project such as furnishing and caring for an aquarium provide focused opportunities for children to plan, dictate, and/or write their plans (using invented and teacher-taught spelling), to draw and write about their activity, to discuss what they are doing, to read nonfiction books for needed information, to work cooperatively with other children, to learn facts in a meaningful context, and to enjoy learning. Skills are taught as needed to accomplish projects.	• Instructional strategies revolve around teacher-directed reading groups that take up most of every morning, lecturing to the whole group, total class discussion, and paper-and-pencil practice exercises or worksheets to be completed silently by children working individually at desks. Projects, learning centers, play, and outdoor time are seen as embellishments and are only offered if time permits or as reward for good behavior.
	• Teachers use much of their planning time to prepare the environment so children can learn through active involvement with each other, with adults and older children serving as informal tutors, and with materials. Many learning centers are available for children to choose from. Many centers include opportunities for writing and reading, for example a tempting library area for browsing through books, reading silently, or sharing a book with a friend; a listening station; and places to practice writing stories and to play math or language games. Teachers encourage children to evaluate their own work and to determine where improvement is needed and assist children in figuring out for themselves how to improve their work. Some work is corrected in small groups where children take turns giving feedback to one another and correcting their own papers. Errors are viewed as a natural and necessary part of learning. Teachers analyze children's errors and use the information obtained to plan curriculum and instruction.	• Teachers use most of their planning time to prepare and correct worksheets and other seatwork. Little time is available to prepare enriching activities, such as those recommended in the teacher's edition of each textbook series. A few interest areas are available for children who finish their seatwork early or children are assigned to a learning center to complete a prescribed sequence of teacher-directed activities within a controlled time period.

Component	APPROPRIATE Practice	INAPPROPRIATE Practice
Teaching strategies *(continued)*	• Individual children or small groups are expected to work and play cooperatively or alone in learning centers and on projects that they usually select themselves or are guided to by the teacher. Activity centers are changed frequently so children have new things to do. Teachers and children together select and develop projects. Frequent outings and visits from resource people are planned. Peer tutoring as well as learning from others through conversation while at work or play occurs daily.	• During most work times, children are expected to work silently and alone on worksheets or other seatwork. Children rarely are permitted to help each other at work time. Penalties for talking are imposed.
	• Learning materials and activities are concrete, real, and relevant to children's lives. Objects children can manipulate and experiment with such as blocks, cards, games, woodworking tools, arts and crafts materials including paint and clay, and scientific equipment are readily accessible. Tables are used for children to work alone or in small groups. A variety of work places and spaces is provided and flexibly used.	• Available materials are limited primarily to books, workbooks, and pencils. Children are assigned permanent desks and desks are rarely moved. Children work in a large group most of the time and no one can participate in a playful activity until all work is finished.

Elisabeth Nichols

Every day, individual children or small groups are expected to work and play cooperatively or alone in learning centers and on projects that they usually select themselves or are guided to by the teacher.

Component	APPROPRIATE Practice	INAPPROPRIATE Practice
Integrated curriculum	• The goals of the language and literacy program are for children to expand their ability to communicate orally and through reading and writing, and to enjoy these activities. Technical skills or subskills are taught as needed to accomplish the larger goals, not as the goal itself. Teachers provide generous amounts of time and a variety of interesting activities for children to develop language, writing, spelling, and reading ability, such as: looking through, reading, or being read high quality children's literature and nonfiction for pleasure and information; drawing, dictating, and writing about their activities or fantasies; planning and implementing projects that involve research at suitable levels of difficulty; creating teacher-made or child-written lists of steps to follow to accomplish a project; discussing what was read; preparing a weekly class newspaper; interviewing various people to obtain information for projects; making books of various kinds (riddle books, *what if* books, books about pets); listening to recordings or viewing high quality films of children's books; being read at least one high quality book or part of a book each day by adults or older children; using the school library and the library area of the classroom regularly. Some children read aloud daily to the teacher, another child, or a small group of children, while others do so weekly. Subskills such as learning letters, phonics, and word recognition are taught as needed to individual children and small groups through enjoyable games and activities. Teachers use the teacher's edition of the basal reader series as a guide to plan projects and hands-on activities relevant to what is read and to structure learning situations. Teachers accept children's invented spelling with minimal reliance on teacher-prescribed spelling lists. Teachers also teach literacy as the need arises when working on science, social studies, and other content areas.	• The goal of the reading program is for each child to pass the standardized tests given throughout the year at or near grade level. Reading is taught as the acquisition of skills and subskills. Teachers teach reading only as a discrete subject. When teaching other subjects, they do not feel they are teaching reading. A sign of excellent teaching is considered to be silence in the classroom and so conversation is allowed infrequently during select times. Language, writing, and spelling instruction are focused on workbooks. Writing is taught as grammar and penmanship. The focus of the reading program is the basal reader, used only in reading groups, and accompanying workbooks and worksheets. The teacher's role is to prepare and implement the reading lesson in the teacher's guidebook for each group each day and to see that other children have enough seatwork to keep them busy throughout the reading group time. Phonics instruction stresses learning rules rather than developing understanding of systematic relationships between letters and sounds. Children are required to complete worksheets or to complete the basal reader although they are capable of reading at a higher level. Everyone knows which children are in the slowest reading group. Children's writing efforts are rejected if correct spelling and standard English are not used.

70

Component	APPROPRIATE Practice	INAPPROPRIATE Practice
Integrated curriculum *(continued)*	• The goal of the math program is to enable children to use math through exploration, discovery, and solving meaningful problems. Math activities are integrated with other relevant projects, such as science and social studies. Math skills are acquired through spontaneous play, projects, and situations of daily living. Teachers use the teacher's edition of the math textbook as a guide to structure learning situations and to stimulate ideas about interesting math projects. Many math manipulatives are provided and used. Interesting board and card, paper-and-pencil, and other kinds of games are used daily. Noncompetitive, impromptu oral "math stumper" and number games are played for practice.	• Math is taught as a separate subject at a scheduled time each day. A math textbook with accompanying workbooks, practice sheets, and board work is the focus of the math program. Teachers move sequentially through the lessons as outlined in the teacher's edition of the text. Seldom is time available for recommended "hands-on" activities. Only children who finish their math seatwork are permitted to use the few math manipulatives and games in the classroom. Timed tests on number facts are given and graded daily. Competition between children or groups of children (boys vs. girls, Row 1 vs. Row 2) is used to motivate children to learn math facts.
	• Social studies themes are identified as the focus of work for extended periods of time. Social studies concepts are learned through a variety of projects and playful activities involving independent research in library books; excursions and interviewing visitors; discussions; the relevant use of language, writing, spelling (invented and teacher-taught), and reading skills; and opportunities to develop social skills such as planning, sharing, taking turns, and working in committees. The classroom is treated as a laboratory of social relations where children explore values and learn rules of social living and respect for individual differences through experience. Relevant art, music, dance, drama, woodworking, and games are incorporated in social studies.	• Social studies instruction is included occasionally after the reading and math programs are completed. Social studies projects, usually related to holidays, consist of completing brief activities from the social studies textbook or reading a commercially developed weekly newspaper and doing the accompanying seatwork.

Elisabeth Nichols

There are many ways to learn to read, write, and spell other than basal readers, workbooks, and spellers.

Component	APPROPRIATE Practice	INAPPROPRIATE Practice
Integrated curriculum *(continued)*	• Discovery science is a major part of the curriculum, building on children's natural interest in the world. Science projects are experimental and exploratory and encourage active involvement of every child. The science program takes advantage of natural phenomena such as the outdoors, and the classroom includes many plants and pets for which children provide care daily. Through science projects and field trips, children learn to plan; to dictate and/or write their plans; to apply thinking skills such as hypothesizing, observing, experimenting, and verifying; and many science facts related to their own experience.	• Science is taught mainly from a single textbook or not at all. Children complete related worksheets on science topics. Science consists of memorizing facts or watching teacher-demonstrated experiments. Field trips occur rarely or not at all. A science area may have a few plants, seashells, or pine cones that have been there many months and are essentially ignored by the children.
	• A variety of health and safety projects (such as nutrition, dental health, handwashing) are designed to help children learn many personalized facts about health and safety; to integrate their learning into their daily habits; to plan and to dictate and/or write their plans; to draw and write about these activities; to read silently and aloud; and to enjoy learning because it is related to their lives.	• Health is taught with the aid of posters and a textbook. A health lesson is scheduled once a week or a unit on health is completed once a year.
	• Art, music, movement, woodworking, drama, and dance (and opportunities for other physical activity) are integrated throughout each day as relevant to the curriculum and as needed for children to express themselves aesthetically and physically and to express ideas and feelings. Specialists work with classroom teachers and children. Children explore and experiment with various art media and forms of music.	• Art, music, and physical education are taught as seperate subjects only once a week. Specialists do not coordinate closely with classroom teachers. Representational art, evaluated for approximations to reality, is emphasized. Children are expected to follow specific directions resulting in identical projects. Crafts substitude for artistic expression.
	• Multicultural and nonsexist activities and materials are provided to enhance individual children's self-esteem and to enrich the lives of all children with respectful acceptance and appreciation of differences and similarities.	• Cultural and other individual differences are ignored. Children are expected to adapt to the dominant culture. The lack of a multicultural component in the curriculum is justified by the homogeneity of the group, ignoring the fact that we live in a diverse society.

Component	APPROPRIATE Practice	INAPPROPRIATE Practice
Integrated curriculum *(continued)*	● Outdoor activity is planned daily so children can develop large muscle skills, learn about outdoor environments, and express themselves freely.	● Outdoor time is limited because it is viewed as interfering with instructional time or, if provided, is viewed as recess (a way for children to use up excess energy).
Guidance of social-emotional development	● Teachers promote prosocial behavior, perseverance, industry, and independence by providing many stimulating, motivating activities; encouraging individual choices; allowing as much time as needed for children to complete work; and ensuring moments of private time alone with the teacher or with a close friend.	● Teachers lecture about the importance of appropriate social behavior and use punishment or deprivations (such as no recess) when children who become restless and bored with seatwork whisper, talk, or wander around or when children dawdle and do not finish their work in the allotted time. Teachers do not have time for private conversations with children and only the most able students finish their work in time for special interests or interaction with other children.
	● Children have many opportunities daily to develop social skills such as helping, cooperating, negotiating, and talking with the person involved to solve interpersonal problems. Teachers facilitate the development of social skills at all times, as part of the curriculum.	● Little time is available for children to practice social skills in the classroom because they are seated and doing silent, individual work or are involved in teacher-directed groups. The only opportunities for social interaction occur on the playground, but the teacher is not present unless it is her playground duty day; therefore, children don't have a consistent, familiar adult to help them with problems.
	● Teachers promote the development of children's consciences and self-control through positive guidance techniques including: setting clear limits in a positive manner; involving children in establishing rules for social living and in problem solving of misbehavior; redirecting children to an acceptable activity; and meeting with an individual child who is having problems or with children and their parents. Teachers maintain their perspective about misbehavior, recognizing that every infraction does not warrant attention and identifying those that can be used as learning opportunities.	● Teachers place themselves in an adversarial role with children, emphasizing their power to reward acceptable behavior and punish unacceptable behavior. Their primary goal is maintaining control of the classroom. Teachers spend considerable time enforcing rules, giving external rewards for good behavior, and punishing infractions. When social conflicts arise, the teacher intervenes, separating and quieting participants, avoiding the social issue. Whether or not the teacher intends, her attitude often feels demeaning to the child.

Component	APPROPRIATE Practice	INAPPROPRIATE Practice
Guidance of social-emotional development *(continued)*	• Teachers limit or contain overexposure to stimulation such as exciting, frightening, or disturbing real or fantasy events (including holidays, television programs or films, overwhelming museum exhibits, and depictions of disasters). When such events occur, teachers help children deal with excitement or fear and express feelings. Teachers know that although schoolchildren can discriminate between fantasy and reality, their capacity for absorbing stimulation is limited. Teachers recognize signs of overstimulation such as when children become silly, overly excited, and carried away in chasing or wrestling; when children try to unduly scare others by relating dramatic accounts of events or experiences; when children are unable to calm down and focus on the activity at hand; or when they become preoccupied with a frightening event. Teachers' strategy is to prevent these behaviors rather than punishing them and to provide an alternative calming activity.	• Teachers are not sensitive to signs of overstimulation in children and treat such demonstrations as misbehavior that must be punished or teachers escalate the situation by encouraging children to release pent-up energy in uncontrolled activity.
Motivation	• Teachers build on children's internal motivation to make sense of the world and acquire competence. The teacher's role is to work with the child in a supportive way toward shared goals, such as reading, writing, learning about the world, exploring science and math, and mastering the rules and skills of sports. Teachers guide individual children to see alternatives, improvements, and solutions.	• Teachers attempt to motivate children through the use of external rewards and punishments. The teacher's role is to correct errors and make sure the child knows the right answer in all subject areas. Teachers reward children for correct answers with stickers or privileges, praise them in front of the group, and hold them up as examples.
	• Through the relationship with the teacher, the child models her or his enthusiasm for learning, identifies with the teacher's attitudes toward conscientious work, and gains in self-motivation.	• The child, sensing that the teacher is struggling to keep her composure and get through the day, identifies with this attitude and emulates it.

Component	APPROPRIATE Practice	INAPPROPRIATE Practice
Motivation *(continued)*	• Teachers point out how good it feels to overcome a hurdle, to try hard to achieve success, and to live up to one's own standards of achievement. The reward for completing a task is an opportunity to try something even more self-challenging, for example "Now that you've finished this book, you can choose another book you want to read."	• Teachers try to motivate children by giving numerical (85%) or letter grades, stickers, gold stars on charts, candy, or privileges such as extra minutes of recess.
Parent-teacher relations	• Teachers view parents as partners in the educational process. Teachers have time for periodic conferences with each child's parents. Parents' visits to school are welcomed at all times and home visits by teachers are encouraged. Teachers listen to parents, seek to understand their goals for their children, and are respectful of cultural and family differences.	• Teachers are not given time for work with parents although many exceptional teachers do it on their own time. Subtle messages convey that schools are for teachers and children, not parents. Teachers view parents' role as carrying out the school's agenda.
	• Members of each child's family are encouraged to help in the classroom (sharing a cultural event or language, telling or reading a story, tutoring, making learning materials or playing games); to help with tasks related to but not occurring within the classroom (sewing costumes, working in the school library); and to assist with decision-making where appropriate.	• Schedules are so tight that parents are seen as one more frustration to teachers who need to cover the curriculum. A policy exists for parent participation, but it receives little time or effort. Teachers go to occasional PTA/PTO meetings and sit quietly in the audience. Teachers make formal contacts with parents through report cards and one yearly conference.
Evaluation	• No letter or numerical grades are given during the primary years. Grades are considered inadequate reflections of children's ongoing learning.	• Grades are seen as important in motivating children to do their work.
	• Each child's progress is assessed primarily through observation and recording at regular intervals. Results are used to improve and individualize instruction. No letter or number grades are given. Children are helped to understand and correct their errors.	• Children are tested regularly on each subject. Graded tests are sent home or are filed after children see their grades. To ease children's stress caused by the emphasis placed on test scores, teachers "teach to the test."
	• Children's progress is reported to parents in the form of narrative comments following an outline of topics. A child's progress is reported in comparison to his or her own previous performance and parents are given general information about how the child compares to standardized national averages.	• Children's progress is reported to parents in letter or numerical grades. Emphasis is on how well the child compares to others in the same grade and to standardized national averages.

75

Component	APPROPRIATE Practice	INAPPROPRIATE Practice
Evaluation (*continued*)	• Children are not "promoted" nor do they "fail." Because children progress through sequential curriculum at different paces, they are allowed to progress in all areas as they acquire competence. Retention is avoided because of its serious impact on children's self-esteem and the fact that the practice of retaining children in a grade for another year disproportionately affects male, minority, very young, and low-income children. The program is designed to serve the needs of the children; the children are not expected to change to fit the program.	• Children repeat a grade or are placed in a special "transition" grade if they have not mastered the expected reading and math skills. It is assumed that their performance will improve with repetition or as they mature. Placement decisions are based on children's ability to sit still and complete paperwork, follow directions, and read at or near grade level.
Grouping and staffing	• Size of classroom groups and ratio of adults to children is carefully regulated to allow active involvement of children and time for teachers to plan and prepare group projects that integrate learning and skills in many subject areas and relate to children's interests; to plan for and work with individual children having special needs or interests; to plan and work with parents; and to coordinate with other teachers, teams of specialists, and administrators involved in each child's school experience. Groups of 5-, 6-, 7-, and 8-year-olds are no larger than 25 with 2 adults, one of whom may be a paraprofessional, or no larger than 15 to 18 with one teacher.	• Groups of 25 to 35 children with one teacher are considered acceptable because they are economical and possible with strict scheduling and discipline, use of prepaced textbooks and workbooks, and devoting little attention to individual needs or interests, allowing minimal parent involvement, and allowing no time for coordination among teachers and specialists. Kindergarten teachers must teach a total of 50 or more children in separate morning and afternoon sessions without the assistance of a paraprofessional.
	• Classroom groups vary in size and composition depending on children's needs. Some groups consist mostly of 5- and 6-year-olds or 6- and 7-year-olds, while others span 3 chronological years (5-, 6-, and 7-year-olds or 6-, 7-, and 8-year-olds) or are composed mainly of same-age children. Children are placed where it is expected that they will do their best, which may be in a family grouping and which is more likely to be determined by developmental than by chronological age. Persistent difficulties of individual children are handled in small groups with more intensive help and the composition of these groups is flexible and temporary.	• Classrooms consist of 25 to 35 children without opportunity for teachers to place children in smaller classes when needed (except children diagnosed as eligible for special or remedial education). Children are grouped by chronological age whenever possible, although inconsistencies arise due to dates of birth and the retention of some children. Children are tracked into homogeneous groups according to ability level.

76

Component	APPROPRIATE Practice	INAPPROPRIATE Practice
Grouping and staffing *(continued)*	• Five- through 8-year-old children are assigned a primary teacher and remain in relatively small groups of 15 to 25 because so much of their learning and development is integrated and cannot be divided into specialized subjects to be taught by special teachers. Specialists assist the primary adult with special projects, questions, and materials.	• Departmentalized settings and groups of 80 or more children with a team of teachers are common. Teachers teach their special areas of interest and what they know best in isolation from one another and children rotate among different teachers.
	• Care is taken to integrate special needs children into the mainstream classroom socially as well as physically. Care is taken to avoid isolating special needs children in a segregated classroom or pulling them out of a regular classroom so often as to disrupt continuity and undermine their feeling of belonging to the group.	• Special needs children are nominally assigned to a regular class, but almost all their instruction occurs with special teachers elsewhere in the building. These children have only a vague sense of what is happening in their regular classroom and the classroom teacher spends little time with them because she assumes they are getting intensive treatment from the special education teacher. Special needs children may be seated together in a designated area of their regular classroom.
Teacher qualifications	• Teachers are qualified to work with 5- through 8-year-olds through Early Childhood Education degree programs or Elementary Education degree programs with a specialty in Early Childhood Education that includes supervised field experience with this age group and required coursework in child development and how children learn, in integrated curriculum and instructional strategies, and in communication with families.	• Elementary or secondary teachers with no specialized training or field experience working with 5- through 8-year-olds are considered qualified because they are state certified regardless of the grade level for which their coursework prepared them.
	• Ongoing professional development opportunities are provided for primary grade teachers to ensure developmentally appropriate curriculum and instruction and to help teachers become more competent, confident, and creative.	• Teachers participate in continuing professional development to maintain certification although development opportunities are not necessarily related to the primary age group.

Component	APPROPRIATE Practice	INAPPROPRIATE Practice
Before- and after-school care	• The before- or after-school program is staffed by people trained in early childhood education, child development, and/or recreation. The program offers a wide variety of choices for children (including nutritious snacks) and features private areas, good books, sports, expeditions, clubs, and many home activities like cooking and woodworking. Children may do homework for a short period of time if they choose.	• The before- or after-school program is staffed by unqualified persons with little or no training in child development or recreation. The before- or after-school program is operated as an extension of the structured school day with children expected to do homework or occupy themselves with paper-and-pencil activities OR the program is considered babysitting and children are warehoused in large groups with few available materials.
Transitions	• Children are assisted in making smooth transitions between groups or programs throughout the day by teachers who provide program continuity, maintain ongoing communication, prepare children for the transition, involve parents, and minimize the number of transitions necessary.	• A child's day is fragmented among many different groups and programs with little attempt by adults to communicate or coordinate successful transitions.

Darla Cole

Good after-school programs offer a wide variety of choices for children (including nutritious snacks) and feature private areas, good books, sports, expeditions, clubs, and many home activities like cooking and woodworking.

References

Asher, S., Hymel, S., & Renshaw, P. (1984). Loneliness in children. *Child Development, 55,* 1456–1464.

Asher, S., Renshaw, P., & Hymel, S. (1982). Peer relations and the development of social skills. In S. Moore & C. Cooper (Eds.), *The young child: Reviews of research* (Vol. 3, pp. 137–158). Washington, DC: NAEYC.

Asher, S. R., & Williams, G. A. (1987). Helping children without friends in home and school contexts. In *Children's social development: Information for teachers and parents* (pp. 1–26). Urbana, IL: ERIC Clearinghouse on Elementary and Early Childhood Education.

Barth, R. S. (1972). *Open education and the American schools.* New York: Agathon Press.

Bennett, W. (1986). *First lessons: A report on elementary education in America.* Washington, DC: U.S. Government Printing Office.

Biber, B., Murphy, L. B., Woodcock, L., Black, I. (1942). *Child life in school: A study of a seven-year-old group.* New York: Dutton.

Blank, M. (1985). Classroom discourse: The neglected topic of the topic. In M. Clark (Ed.), *Helping communication in early education* (pp. 13–20). Education Review Occasional Publication No. 11.

Burton, C. B. (1987). Children's peer relationships. In *Children's social development: Information for teachers and parents* (pp. 27–34). Urbana, IL: ERIC Clearinghouse on Elementary and Early Childhood Education.

Covington, M. V. (1984). The motive for self worth. In R. Ames & C. Ames (Eds.), *Research on motivation in education: Vol. 1. Student motivation* (pp. 78–113). New York: Academic.

Cowen, E., Pederson, A., Babigian, M., Izzo, L., & Trost, M. (1973). Long-term follow-up of early detected vulnerable children. *Journal of Consulting and Clinical Psychology, 41,* 438–446.

Dewey, J. (1899). *School and society.* New York: The University of Chicago Press.

Durkin, D. (1980). *Teaching young children to read.* Boston: Allyn & Bacon.

Dweck, C. (1986). Motivational processes affecting learning. *American Psychologist, 41,* 1040–1048.

Elkind, D. (1981). *Children and adolescents: Interpretive essays on Jean Piaget.* New York: Oxford University Press.

Elkind, D. (1987). *Miseducation: Preschoolers at risk.* New York: Knopf.

Erikson, E. (1963). *Childhood and society.* New York: Norton.

Furman, E. (1980). Early latency: Normal and pathological aspects. In S. Greenspan & G. Pollock (Eds.), *The course of life: Vol. 2. Latency, adolescence and youth* (pp. 1–32). Washington, DC: National Institute of Mental Health, U.S. Department of Health and Human Services.

Furman, E. (1987a). *Helping young children grow: I never knew parents did so much.* Madison, CT: International Universities Press.

Furman, E. (1987b). *The teacher's guide to helping young children grow.* Madison, CT: International Universities Press.

Gottfried, A. (1983). Intrinsic motivation in young children. *Young Children, 39*(1), 64–73.

Gronlund, N., & Holmlund, W. (1985). The value of elementary school sociometric status scores for predicting pupils' adjustment in high school. *Educational Administration and Supervision, 44,* 225–260.

Hilliard, A. (1986). Standardized testing in early childhood programs. Unpublished paper.

Hills, T. (1986). *Classroom motivation: Helping students want to learn and achieve in school.* Trenton: New Jersey Department of Education.

Kamii, C. (1985). Leading primary education toward excellence: Beyond worksheets and drill. *Young Children, 40*(6), 3–9.

Katz, L. (1985). Dispositions in early childhood education. *ERIC/EECE Bulletin, 18*(2), 1, 3.

Katz, L., & Chard, S. (in press). *Engaging the minds of young children: The project approach.* Norwood, NJ: Ablex.

Katz, L., Raths, J., & Torres, R. (undated). *A place called kindergarten.* Urbana, IL: ERIC Clearinghouse on Elementary and Early Childhood Education.

Nelson, K. (1985). *Making sense: The acquisition of shared meaning.* New York: Academic.

Office of Educational Research and Improvement. (1986). *Becoming a nation of readers: Implications for teachers.* Washington, DC: U.S. Department of Education.

Parker, J., & Asher, S. (1986, March). *Predicting later outcomes from peer rejection: Studies of school drop out, delinquency, and adult psychopathology.* Paper presented at the annual conference of the American Educational Research Association, San Francisco. In press: *Psychological Bulletin.*

Piaget, J. (1952). *The child's conception of number.* London: Routledge & Kegan Paul.

Piaget, J., & Inhelder, B. (1969). *The psychology of the child.* New York: Basic.

Schweinhart, L., Weikart, D., & Larner, M. (1986). Consequences of three preschool curriculum models through age 15. *Early Childhood Research Quarterly, 1*(1), 15–46.

Stipek, D. (1984). The development of achievement motivation. In R. Ames & C. Ames (Eds.), *Research on motivation in education: Vol. 1. Student motivation* (pp. 145–174). New York: Academic.

Van Deusen-Henkel, J., & Argondizza, M. (1987). Early elementary education: Curriculum planning for the primary grades. In *A framework for curriculum design: People, process, and product.* Augusta, ME: Division of Curriculum, Maine Department of Educational and Cultural Services.

Walberg, H. (1984). Improving the productivity of America's schools. *Educational Leadership, 41*(8), 19–30.

Weber, L. (1971). *The British Infant School and informal education.* Englewood Cliffs, NJ: Prentice-Hall.

Wells, G. (1983). Talking with children: The complementary roles of parents and teachers. In M. Donaldson, R. Grieve, & C. Pratt (Eds.), *Early childhood development and education* (pp. 127–150). New York: Guilford.

Wilkinson, L. (1984). Research currents: Peer group talk in elementary school. *Language Arts, 61*(2), 164–169.

Selected bibliography (See also references and bibliography pp. 14–16.)

Aesthetic development

Barden, M. (1985). From Snoopy to Matisse. *Instructor, 45*(1), 20–24.

Brittain, W. L. (1979). *Creativity, art, and the young child.* New York: Macmillan.

Burton, L., & Hughes, W. (1981). *Musicplay.* Menlo Park, CA: Addison-Wesley.

Burton, L., & Kuroda, K. (1979). *Artsplay.* Menlo Park, CA: Addison-Wesley.

Carpenter, J. (1986). *Creating the world: Poetry, art, and children.* Seattle: University of Washington Press.

Getty Center for Education in the Arts. (1985). *Beyond creating: The place for art in America's schools.* Santa Monica, CA: Rand Corporation.

Hitz, R. (1987). Creative problem solving through music activities. *Young Children, 42*(2), 12–17.

Hubbard, R. (1987). Transferring images: Not just glued on the page. *Young Children, 42*(2), 60–67.

Kellogg, R. (1969–70). *Analyzing children's art.* Palo Alto, CA: National Press Books.

Lanier, V. (1983). *The visual arts and the elementary child.* New York: Teachers College Press, Columbia University.

Lasky, L., & Mukerji, R. (1980). *Art: Basic for young children.* Washington, DC: NAEYC.

Levy, V. (1983). *Let's go to the art museum.* Pompano Beach, FL: Veejay Publications.

McDonald, D. (1979). *Music in our lives: The early years.* Washington, DC: NAEYC.

Milbrey, W., Thomas, M., & Peterson, J. (1984). *Art history, art criticism, and art production: An examination of art education in selected school districts. Vol. 3. Executive summary.* Santa Monica, CA: Rand Corporation.

Schirrmacher, R. (1986). Talking with young children about their art. *Young Children, 41*(5), 3–7.

Smith, N. (1983). *Experience and art: Teaching children to paint.* New York: Teachers College Press, Columbia University.

Sullivan, M. L. (1982). *Feeling strong, feeling free: Movement exploration for young children.* Washington, DC: NAEYC.

Townley, M. (1978). *Another look.* Menlo Park, CA: Addison-Wesley.

Assessment of children

Bailey, D. B. & Harvin, G. L. (1980). Nondiscriminatory evaluation. *Exceptional Children, 46*(8), 590–596.

Brandt, R. S. (Ed.). (1989). Redirecting assessment [special issue]. *Educational Leadership, 46*(7).

Bredekamp, S., & Shepard, L. (1989). How best to protect children from inappropriate school expectations, practices and policies. *Young Children, 44*(3), 14–24.

Glaser, R. (1981). The future of testing. *American Psychologist, 36*(9), 923–936.

Goodwin, W. L., & Driscoll, L. A. (1980). *Handbook for measurement and evaluation in early childhood.* San Francisco: Jossey-Bass.

Hills, T. (1986). Screening for school entry. *ERIC/EECE Bulletin, 18*(4), 1–4.

Kamii, C. (Ed.). (in press). *Achievement testing in the early grades: Games grown-ups play.* Washington, DC: NAEYC.

Meisels, S. J. (1985). *Developmental screening in early childhood: A guide.* Washington, DC: NAEYC.

Meisels, S. J. (1987). Uses and abuses of developmental screening and school readiness testing. *Young Children, 42*(2) 4–6, 68–73.

National Association for the Education of Young Children. (1988). NAEYC position statement on standardized testing of young children 3 through 8 years of age. *Young Children, 43*(3), 42–47.

National Association of School Psychologists. (1988). *Student grade retention.* Washington, DC: Author.

Perrone, V. (1976). On standardized testing and evaluation. *Childhood Education, 53*(1), 9–15.

Before- and after-school care

Alexander, N. P. (1986). School-age child care: Concerns and challenges. *Young Children, 42*(1), 3–10.

Baden, R., Genser, A., Leving, J., & Seligson, M. (1982). *School-age child care: An action manual.* Dover, MA: Auburn House.

Blau, R., Brady, E. H., Bucher, I., Hiteshew, B., Zavitkovsky, A., & Zavitkovsky, D. (1977). *Activities for school-age child care.* Washington, DC: NAEYC.

Genser, A., & Baden, C. (Eds.). (1980). *School-age child care: Programs and issues.* Urbana, IL: ERIC Clearinghouse on Elementary and Early Childhood Education.

Nieting, P. S. (1983). School-age child care: In support of developmental learning. *Childhood Education, 60*(1), 6–11.

Powell, D. R. (1987). Research in review. After-school child care. *Young Children, 42*(3), 62–66.

Seligson, M., Genser, A., Gannett, E., & Gray, W. (1983). *School-age child care: A policy report.* School-Age Child Care Project, Center for Research on Women, Wellesley College, Wellesley, MA 02181.

Cognitive development

Athey, I., & Rubadeau, O. (1973). *Educational implications of Piaget's theory.* Waltham, MA: Xerox College Publishing.

Donaldson, M. (1978). *Children's minds.* Glasgow: Fontana.

Donaldson, M., Grieve, R., & Pratt, C. (Eds.). (1983). *Early childhood development and education.* New York: Guilford.

Forman, G., & Kuschner, D. (1983). *The child's construction of knowledge: Piaget for teaching children.* Washington, DC: NAEYC.

Goffin, S. G., & Tull, C. Q. (1985). Problem solving: Encouraging active learning. *Young Children, 40*(3), 28–32.

Hirsh, E. S. (Ed.). (1984). *The block book* (rev. ed.). Washington, DC: NAEYC.

Just think: Program 1. K–1. Thomas Geale Publishing Company, Inc., Drawer C.P. 223, 1142 Manhattan Ave., Manhattan Beach, CA 90266.

Just think: Program 2. 1–2. Thomas Geale Publishing Company, Inc., Drawer C.P. 223, 1142 Manhattan Ave., Manhattan Beach, CA 90266.

Just think: Program 3. 2–3. Thomas Geale Publishing Company, Inc., Drawer C.P. 223, 1142 Manhattan Ave., Manhattan Beach, CA 90266.

Piaget, J. (1970). *Science and education and the psychology of the child.* New York: Orion Press.

Piaget, J. (1973). *To understand is to invent.* New York: Grossman.

Reifel, S. (1984). Block construction: Children's developmental landmarks in representation of space. *Young Children, 40*(1), 61–67.

Sigel, I., & Cocking, R. (1977). *Cognitive development from childhood to adolescence: A constructivist perspective.* New York: Holt, Rinehart & Winston.

Wadsworth, B. (1978). *Piaget for the classroom teacher.* New York: Longman.

Williams, C. K., & Kamii, C. (1986). How do children learn by handling objects? *Young Children, 42*(1), 23–26.

Young think. PreK–K. Thomas Geale Publishing Company, Inc., Drawer C.P. 223, 1142 Manhattan Ave., Manhattan Beach, CA 90266.

General development

Bee, H. (1985). *The developing child* (4th ed.). New York: Harper & Row.

Collins, W. A. (1984). *Development during middle childhood.* Washington, DC: National Academy Press.

Williams, J., & Stith, M. (1980). *Middle childhood: Behavior and development.* New York: Macmillan.

Grouping

Cole, J. (1985, January). Is seven the perfect age? *Parents,* pp. 60–65.

Cook, G., & Stammer, J. (1985). Grade retention and social promotion practices. *Childhood Education, 61*(4), 302–308.

Doremus, V. P. (1986). Forcing works for flowers, but not for children. *Educational Leadership, 44*(3), 32–35

Dunn, N. E. (1981). Children's achievement at school-entry age as a function of mothers' and fathers' teaching sets. *Elementary School Journal, 81,* 245–253.

Featherstone, H (1987). Organizing classes by ability. *The Harvard Education Newsletter, 3*(4), 1–4.

Goodlad, J., & Anderson, R. (1987). *Nongraded elementary school* (2nd ed.). New York: Teachers College Press, Columbia University.

Roberts, C. M. L. (1986). Whatever happened to kindergarten? *Educational Leadership, 44*(3), 34.

Shepard, L. A., & Smith, M. L. (1986). Synthesis of research on school readiness and kindergarten retention. *Educational Leadership, 44*(3), 78–86.

Slavin, R. (1986). *Ability grouping and student achievement in elementary schools: A best evidence synthesis.* Baltimore: Center for Research on Elementary and Middle Schools, The Johns Hopkins University, 3505 N. Charles St., Baltimore, MD 21218.

Smith, M. L., & Shepard, L. A. (1987). What doesn't work: Explaining policies of retention in the early grades. *Phi Delta Kappan, 67,* 129–134.

Smith, M. L., & Shepard, L. A. (1988). Kindergarten readiness and retention: A qualitative study of teachers' beliefs and practices. *American Educational Research Journal, 25*(3), 307–333.

Webster, N. K. (1984). The 5's and 6's go to school, revisited. *Childhood Education, 60,* 325–330.

Language and literacy

Atkins, C. (1984). Writing: Doing something constructive. *Young Children, 40*(1), 3–7.

Bailey, M. H., Durkin, D., Nurss, J. R., & Stammer, J. D. (1982). Preparation of kindergarten teachers for reading instruction. *The Reading Teacher, 36,* 307–311.

Barbour, N., Webster, T. D., & Drosdeck, S. (1987). Sand: A resource for the language arts. *Young Children, 42*(2), 20–25.

Bridge, C. A., Winograd, P. N., & Haley, D. (1983). Using predictable materials vs. primers. *The Reading Teacher, 36,* 884–891.

Brown, M. H., Weinberg, S. H., & Cromer, P. S. (1986). Kindergarten children coming to literacy. *Educational Leadership, 44*(3), 54–56.

Chomsky, C. (1974). *Invented spelling in first grade.* Paper presented at Reading Research Symposium, State University of New York at Buffalo.

Connell, D. R. (1985). *Writing is child's play.* Circle Pines, MN: American Guidance Service.

Connell, D. R. (1983). Handwriting: Taking a look at the alternatives. *Academic Therapy, 18,* 413–420.

Durkin, D. (1966). *Children who read early.* New York: Teachers College Press, Columbia University.

Durkin, D. (1987). *Teaching young children to read* (4th ed.). Boston: Allyn & Bacon.

Faber, A., & Mazlish, E. (1982). *How to talk so kids will listen and listen so kids will talk.* New York: Avon.

Fields, M. (1987). *Let's begin reading right: A developmental approach to beginning literacy.* Columbus, OH: Merrill.

Fox, S., & Allen, V. G. (1983). *The language arts: An integrated approach.* New York: Holt, Rinehart & Winston.

Gentile, L. M., & Hoot, J. L. (1983). Kindergarten play: The foundation of reading. *The Reading Teacher, 36,* 436–439.

Graves, D. H. (1979). Let children show us how to help them write. *Visible Language, 13*(1), 16–28.

Graves, D. H. (1983). *Writing: Teachers and children at work.* Portsmouth, NH: Heinemann.

Hall, M. A. (1981). *Teaching reading as a language experience* (3rd ed.). Columbus, OH: Merrill.

Holdaway, D. (1979). *The foundation of literacy.* Portsmouth, NH: Heinemann.

Irwin, D. M., & Bushnell, M. M. (1980). *Observational strategies for child study.* New York: Holt, Rinehart & Winston.

Jewell, M. G. & Zintz, M. V. (1986). *Learning to read naturally.* Dubuque, IA: Kendall/Hunt.

Karnowski, L. (1986). How young writers communicate. *Educational Leadership, 44*(3), 58–60.

National Council of Teachers of English Commission on Reading. (1988). *Basal readers and the state of American reading instruction: A call for action* (position statement). Urbana, IL: Author.

National Council of Teachers of English Commission on Reading. (1988). *Report on basal readers* (position statement). Urbana, IL: Author.

National Institute of Education. (1984). *Becoming a nation of readers.* Washington, DC: U.S. Office of Education.

Pflaum, S. (1986). *The development of language and literacy in young children* (3rd ed.). Columbus, OH: Merrill.

Ringler, L., & Weber, C. (1984). *A language-thinking approach to reading.* New York: Harcourt Brace Jovanovich.

Schickedanz, J. (1986). *More than the ABC's: The early stages of reading and writing.* Washington DC: NAEYC.

Taylor, D. (1983). *Family literacy: Young children learning to read and write.* Portsmouth, NH: Heinemann.

Teale, W. H. (1978). Positive environments for learning to read: What studies of early readers tell us. *Language Arts, 55*, 922—932).

Teale, W. H. & Sulzby, E. (1986). *Emergent literacy: Writing and reading.* Norwood, NJ: Ablex.

Willert, M. K. & Kamii, C. (1985). Reading in kindergarten: Direct vs. indirect teaching. *Young Children, 40*(4), 3–9.

Mathematics

Berman, B. (1982).How children learn math: Rediscovering manipulatives. *Curriculum Review, 21*, 192–196.

Burns, M. (1987, January). Why California said NO to 14 math text book series. *Learning*, pp. 50–51.

Copeland, R. (1974). *Diagnostic and learning activities in mathematics for children.* New York: Macmillan.

Copeland, R. (1974). *How children learn mathematics* (2nd ed.). New York: Macmillan.

Dienes, Z. (1971). *Building up mathematics.* London: Hutchinson Educational.

Dienes, Z., & Golding, E. (1973). *Modern mathematics for young children.* New York: McGraw-Hill.

Ginsburg, H. (1982). *Children's arithmetic: How they learn it and how you teach it.* Austin, TX: Pro-Ed.

Ginsburg, H. (Ed.). (1983). *The development of mathematical thinking.* New York: Academic.

Henninger, M. (1987). Learning mathematics through play. *Childhood Education, 63*(3), 167–171.

Kamii, C. (1982). *Number in preschool and kindergarten.* Washington, DC: NAEYC.

Kamii, C. (1985). *Young children reinvent arithmetic.* New York: Teachers College Press, Columbia University.

Kamii, C., & DeVries, R. (1980). *Group games in early education: Implications of Piaget's theory.* Washington, DC: NAEYC.

Kunz, J. (1965). *Modern mathematics made meaningful with Cuisenaire rods.* Cuisenaire Company of America, 12 Church St., P.O. Box D, New Rochelle, NY 10802.

Lavatelli, C. (1973). *Early childhood curriculum: A Piaget program. Teacher's guide.* American Science and Engineering, Fort Washington, Cambridge, MA 02139.

McCracken, J. B. (1987). *More than 1,2,3,: The real basics of mathematics.* Washington, DC: NAEYC.

National Council of Teachers of Mathematics. (1980). *An agenda for action: Recommendations for school mathematics of the 1980s.* Reston, VA: Author.

National Council of Teachers of Mathematics. (1989). *Curriculum and evaluation standards for school mathematics.* Reston, VA: Author.

O'Hara, E. (1975, October). Piaget: The six-year-old and modern math. *Today's Education,* pp. 32–36.

Skeen, P., Garner, A. P., & Cartwright, S. *Woodworking for young children.* Washington, DC: NAEYC.

Stern, C., & Stern, M. B. (1971). *Children discover arithmetic.* New York: Harper & Row.

Moral development

Cryan, J. (1987). The banning of corporal punishment in child care, school and other educational settings (a position paper). *Childhood Education, 63*(3), 146–153.

Gartrell, D. (1987). Assertive discipline: Unhealthy for children and other living things. *Young Children, 42*(2), 10–11.

Gartrell, D. (1987). Punishment or guidance? *Young Children, 42*(3), 55–61.

Honig, A. S. (1985). Research in review. Compliance, control, and discipline. Part 1. *Young Children, 40*(2), 50–58.

Honig, A. S. (1985). Research in review. Compliance, control, and discipline. Part 2. *Young Children, 40*(3), 47–52.

Ideas That Work With Young Children. (1987). Good discipline is, in large part, the result of a fantastic curriculum! *Young Children, 42*(3), 49–51.

Kohlberg, L. (1987). *Child psychology and early education.* New York: Longman.

Krogh, S. L., & Lamme, L. L. (1985). "But what about sharing?" Children's literature and moral development. *Young Children, 40*(4), 48–51.

Miller, C. S. (1984). Building self-control: Discipline for young children. *Young Children, 40*(1), 15–19.

Riley, S. S. (1984). *How to generate values in young children: Integrity, honesty, individuality, self-confidence, and wisdom.* Washington, DC: NAEYC.

Stone, J. G. (1978). *A guide to discipline.* Washington, DC: NAEYC.

Weber-Schwartz, N. (1987). Patience or understanding? *Young Children, 42*(3), 52–54.

Parent-teacher relations

Becher, R. M. (1985). Parent involvement and reading achievement: A review of research. *Childhood Education, 62*(1), 44–50.

Bjorklund, G., & Burger, C. (1987). Making conferences work for parents, teachers, and children. *Young Children, 42*(2), 26–31.

Hymes, J. L., Jr. (1975). *Effective home-school relations* (rev. ed.). Hacienda Press, P.O. Box 222415, Carmel, CA 93922.

Lightfoot, S. (1978). *Worlds apart.* New York: Basic.

Lyons, P., Robbins, A., & Smith, A. (1983). *Involving parents: A handbook for participation in schools.* Ypsilanti, MI: High/Scope.

Honig, A. S. (1979). *Parent involvement in early childhood education.* Washington, DC: NAEYC.

Powell, D. R. (1986). Research in review. Parent education and support programs. *Young Children, 41*(3), 47–53.

Readdick, C. A., Golbeck, S. L., Klein, E. L., & Cartwright, C. A. (1984). The child-parent-teacher conference: A setting for child development. *Young Children, 39*(5), 67–73.

Playgrounds

Coleman, M., & Skeen, P. (1985). Play, games, and sport: Their use and misuse. *Childhood Education, 61*(3), 192–198.

Churchman, A. (Ed.). (1986). Schoolyards [Special issue]. *Children's Environmental Quarterly, 3*(3).

Frost, J., & Klein, B. (1979). *Children's play and playgrounds.* Boston: Allyn & Bacon.

Frost, J. L., & Sunderlin, S. (Eds.). (1985). *When children play.* Wheaton, MD: Association for Childhood Education International.

Ideas That Work With Young Children. (1985). Outdoor games. *Young Children, 40*(5), 14.

Science

Carlin, A. A., & Sund, R. B. (1980). *Teaching science through discovery.* Columbus, Ohio: Merrill.

Diamond, D. (1979). *Introduction and guide to teaching primary science.* Milwaukee: McDonald-Raintree.

Gega, P. (1986). *Science in elementary education* (5th ed.). New York: Wiley.

Holt, B. (1977). *Science with young children.* Washington, DC: NAEYC.

Kamii, C., & DeVries, R. (1978). *Physical knowledge in preschool education.* Englewood Cliffs, NJ: Prentice-Hall.

Link, M. (1981). *Outdoor education: A manual for teaching in nature's classroom.* Englewood Cliffs, NJ: Prentice-Hall.

McIntyre, M. (1984). *Early childhood and science.* Washington, DC: National Science Teachers Association.

Papert, S. (1980). *Mindstorms: Children, computers, and powerful ideas.* New York: Basic.

Robinson, B., & Wilson, E. (1982). *Environmental education: A manual for elementary educators.* New York: Teachers College Press, Columbia University.

Rowe, M. B. (1982). *Education in the eighties: Science.* Washington, DC: National Education Association.

Rowe, M. B. (1978). *Teaching science as continuous inquiry.* New York: McGraw-Hill.

Trojcak, D. A. (1979). *Science with children.* New York: McGraw-Hill.

Social studies

Borden, E. J. (1987). The community connection—It works! *Young Children, 42*(4), 14–23.

National Council for the Social Studies. (1989). Social studies for early childhood and elementary school children preparing for the 21st century: A report from NCSS task force on early childhood/elementary social studies. *Social Education, 53*(1), 14–24.

Pagano, A. (1978). *Social studies in early childhood. An interactionist point of view.* Washington, DC: National Council for the Social Studies.

Ryan, F. (1980). *The social studies sourcebook.* Boston: Allyn & Bacon.

Saracho, O. N., & Spodek, B. (1983). *Understanding the multicultural experience in early childhood education.* Washington, DC: NAEYC.

Seefeldt, C. (1984). *Social studies for the preschool-primary child* (2nd ed.). Columbus, OH: Merrill.

Smith, C. (1982). *Promoting the social development of young children: Strategies and activities.* Palo Alto, CA: Mayfield.

Social-emotional development (See also references)

Bryant, B. K. (1985). The neighborhood walk: Sources of support in middle childhood. *Monographs of the Society for Research in Child Development, 50*(3, Serial No. 210).

Damon, W. (1979). *The social world of the child.* San Francisco: Jossey-Bass.

Damon, W. (1983). *Social and personality development.* New York: Norton.

Erikson, E. (1963). *Childhood and society.* New York: Norton.

Goffin, S. G. (1987). Cooperative behaviors: They need our support. *Young Children, 42*(2), 75–81.

Honig, A. S. (1987). Research in review. The shy child. *Young Children, 42*(4), 54–64.

Honig, A. S. (1986). Research in review. Stress and coping in children. Part 1. *Young Children, 41*(4), 50–63.

Honig, A. S. (1986). Research in review. Stress and coping in children. Part 2. *Young Children, 41*(5), 47–59.

Kostelnik, M. J., Whiren, A. P., & Stein, L. C. (1986). Living with He-Man: Managing superhero fantasy play. *Young Children, 41*(4), 3–9.

McCracken, J. B. (Ed.). (1986). *Reducing stress in young children's lives.* Washington DC: NAEYC.

Overton, W. (Ed.). (1985). *The relation between social and cognitive development.* Hillsdale, NJ: Erlbaum.

Rogers, D. L., & Ross, D. D. (1986). Encouraging positive social interaction among young children. *Young Children, 41*(3), 12–17.

Roopnarine, J. L., & Honig, A. S. (1985). Research in review. The unpopular child. *Young Children, 40*(6), 59–64.

Smith, C. A. (1986). Nurturing kindness through storytelling. *Young Children, 41*(6), 46–51.

Warren, R. M. (1977). *Caring: Supporting children's growth.* Washington, DC: NAEYC.

Special needs

Hanline, M. F. (1985). Integrating disabled children. *Young Children, 40*(2), 45–48.

Seefeldt, C. (Ed.). (1983). New arrivals [Special issue]. *Childhood Education, 60*(2).

White, B. P., & Phair, M. A. (1986). "It'll be a challenge!" Managing emotional stress in teaching disabled children. *Young Children, 41*(2), 44–48.

Teacher-child relationships

Ideas That Work With Young Children. (1987). Integrating individualizing into your program. *Young Children, 42*(2), 18–19, 74.

Ideas That Work With Young Children. (1986). The take-a-minute teacher. *Young Children, 42*(1), 21–22.

Klass, C. S. (1987). Childrearing interactions within developmental home- or center-based early education. *Young Children, 42*(3), 9–13, 67–70.

Soderman, A. K. (1985). Dealing with difficult young children: Strategies for teachers and parents. *Young Children, 40*(5), 15–19.

Wardle, F. (1987). Are you sensitive to interracial children's special identity needs? *Young Children, 42*(2), 53–59.

Wolf, D. P. (1986). *Connecting: Friendship in the lives of young children and their teachers.* Richmond, WA: Exchange Press, Inc.

Teaching strategies

Ashton-Warner, S. (1986). *Teacher.* New York: Simon & Schuster.

Aspy, D., & Roebuck, F. (1977). *Kids don't learn from people they don't like.* Amherst, MA: Human Development Press.

Barbour, N. (1987). Curriculum concepts and priorities. *Childhood Education, 63*(5), 331–336.

Bloom, B. S. (1984). The search for methods of group instruction as effective as one to one tutoring. *Educational Leadership, 41*(8), 4–17.

Day, B. D., & Drake, K. N. (1983). *Early childhood education: Curriculum organization and classroom management.* Alexandria, VA: Association for Supervision and Curriculum Development.

Elkind, D. (1986). Formal education and early childlhood education: An essential difference. *Phi Delta Kappan, 67,* 631–636.

Hosford, P. L. (1978). The silent curriculum: Its impact on teaching the basics. *Educational Leadership, 36,* 211–215.

Hosford, P. L. (Ed.). (1984). *Using what we know about teaching.* Alexandria, VA: Association for Supervision and Curriculum Development.

Jackson, P. (1986). *The practice of teaching.* New York: Teachers College Press, Columbia University.

Joyce, B., & Weil, M. (1979). *Models of teaching* (2nd ed.). Englewood Cliffs, NJ: Prentice-Hall.

Lay-Dopyera, M., & Dopyfera, J. (1986). Strategies for teaching. In C. Seefeldt (Ed.), *Early childhood curriculum: A review of current research.* New York: Teachers College Press, Columbia University.

Lieberman, A., & Miller, L. (1984). *Teachers, their world, and their work.* Alexandria, VA: Association for Supervision and Curriculum Development.

McGarry, T. P. (1986). Integrating learning for young children. *Educational Leadership, 44*(3), 64–66.

National Commission on Excellence in Education. (1983, April). *A nation at risk: The imperative for educational reform.* Washington, DC: U.S. Government Printing Office.

Plowden, B., et al. (1966). *Children and their primary schools: A report on the Central Advisory Council for Education.* London: Her Majesty's Stationery Office.

Raths, J., Wasserman, S., Jonas, A., & Rothstein, A. (1986). *Teaching for thinking: Theory, strategy, and activities for the classroom.* New York: Teachers College Press, Columbia University.

Rosenshine, B. V. (1986). Synthesis of research on explicit teaching. *Educational Leadership, 43*(7), 66–69.

Spodek, B. (1988). Conceptualizing today's kindergarten curriculum. *The Elementary School Journal, 89*(2), 203–212.

Williams, C. R., & Heck, S. (1984). *The complex roles of the teacher.* New York: Teachers College Press, Columbia University.

U.S. Department of Education. (1986). *What works: Research about teaching and learning.* Washington, DC: Author.

PART 8

Informing Others About Developmentally Appropriate Practice

Janet K. Black and Margaret B. Puckett

Ann Simpson drops 8-month-old Jennifer at the child care center. Ann excitedly tells Jennifer's caregiver about a newspaper article she read describing a program that teaches babies to read. As she leaves the center, she stops by the director's office to request that this program be implemented in their center.

Maria Lopez is a prekindergarten teacher in a public school program for 4-year-olds. After observing in her room, Maria's principal asks her, "When are you going to start teaching the children? All they do is play."

James Washington teaches second grade in an urban school. He has arranged the children's desks into clusters so they can talk as they work together on projects. They may also choose from among several learning centers in the classroom. The teacher across the hall from James informs him that children learn best in quiet classrooms and that the children should learn to stay in their seats. She warns him that his students will not do well on achievement tests and will not be ready for third grade.

The above vignettes reflect some of the comments early childhood educators hear from parents, administrators, and other teachers about developmentally appropriate practice. Adults who teach in developmentally appropriate ways may feel intimidated and pressured by such statements. A more constructive reaction is to examine reasons why parents, administrators, and other teachers might make these comments.

The purpose of this chapter is to develop understanding about the basis for comments some adults make about developmentally appropriate practice and to provide strategies for using the information in this publication to inform others about developmentally appropriate practice.

Understanding parents

Virtually all parents want the best for their children. They want them to get off to a good start so they will succeed in life. Many parents now realize that the early years are important for later learning. However, most parents do not fully understand how young children learn. They do not equate child-initiated activity and spontaneous play with learning or cognitive development. Their first memory of school is of learning in the elementary grades. They remember structured lessons and rigid routines and assume that such practices are necessary for learning to occur. Some parents who attended nursery school may only remember snack time, rest time, and outdoor play. A typical comment may be, "When I was in preschool all we did was play. I want Jeremy to learn."

Parents make negative comments about developmentally appropriate practice and pressure teachers into inappropriate practices for several reasons. All these reasons are motivated by wanting the best for their children. One reason is economic pressure. Working parents or single parents may feel guilty about not being able to spend as much time with their children as they would like. They may be comforted knowing that their child care center or school is providing an academic environment.

Another reason for parental pressure for formal instruction relates to parents' own needs for self-esteem. All parents have difficulty being objective about their children. Some parents measure their own worth by their children's accomplishments and their social status by their child's enrollment in a "select" school. Some parents want their children to accomplish what they did not. At times, grandparents' expectations and competition between siblings and cousins can contribute to the pressure.

These factors are exacerbated by the media. Through television, newspapers, and magazines parents are bombarded by confusing and conflicting messages about what is appropriate for young children and what they should do to help their children learn. Children's exposure to the media also plays a part. Because children have access to expanded information about the world through the media, parents assume that they fully understand what is presented and that they are ready for more abstract learning.

Finally, early childhood programs themselves are extremely diverse with many emphasizing highly structured, academic curricula that other early childhood professionals would find inappropriate. The array of choices is confusing to parents deciding about a program for their child.

Early childhood educators must recognize the potential causes for parents' negative responses to developmentally appropriate practice and avoid becoming defensive. Parents should be acknowledged for their legitimate desire to be good parents and to provide the best experiences for their children. Early childhood educators must assume the responsibility for understanding and articulating developmentally appropriate practices to parents.

Understanding administrators

Directors, supervisors, curriculum specialists, and principals play important leadership roles in early childhood programs. In some cases, administrators have only recently begun serving younger children in their programs. For example, prekindergarten or kindergarten may be new additions to public schools; infants and toddlers may have been added to a child care center that previously served only preschoolers.

Administrators in these situations probably rely on their own education and experience. Many individuals in leadership positions may have had little or no classroom experience as teachers of young children. Their knowledge may be based on elementary school classrooms designed for older children.

Administrators, even more so than teachers, are pressured to ensure that children learn in their programs. Parents exert heavy pressure on administrators. Commercial curriculum developers influence administrators to purchase kits or textbooks that they claim will help children excel. But most importantly, public school administrators are required to implement various policies mandated by the local school system or state. Accountability requires that school districts use standardized testing to document children's achievement, despite the fact that such testing is often inappropriate for younger children. Pressure to produce higher test scores leads teachers to use more formal instructional methods and "teach to the test." In addition, some teacher evaluation instruments are designed to be used in classrooms where teacher-directed, whole-group instruction is taking place. Thus, principals may pressure teachers of young children to modify their teaching strategies to increase their chances of performing at a higher level on an appraisal instrument.

Administrators need to be understood. Their perspective is based on their educational background and the realities of their position. Early childhood professionals need to be aware of these concerns and work with individuals in leadership positions to ensure that developmentally appropriate practices are accepted and adopted.

Understanding teachers

The increase in early childhood programs over the last 25 years has lead to a shortage of qualified teachers who are prepared to work with young children. Too few colleges and universities have programs that are specifically designed to prepare early childhood educators. As a result, teachers who have had little or no training or who are trained and experienced in working with children in the upper grades may be hired to work with young children.

Many of the same factors influencing parents and pressuring administrators also affect teachers. Specifically, media references to the inadequacy of teachers and the need for school reform undermine teachers' competency. Such indictments contribute to the notion that teachers are not qualified and do not know what they are doing.

Teacher accountability and evaluation may encourage teachers to adopt more formal learning strategies in their early childhood classrooms. Despite the fact that standardized tests are limited in their ability to adequately document the learning that takes place in the early years, their use has become more common. Teachers at primary grade levels often feel a great deal of pressure to cover material for their children to perform well on tests.

Teachers whose classrooms are more structured may be intimidated or threatened by more informal teaching strategies. They may not fully understand developmentally appropriate practices. Early childhood educators should understand the differences in teacher preparation, and the pressures teachers face, and use this understanding as a foundation for improved communication with colleagues.

The lack of understanding about developmentally appropriate practices on the part of many parents, teachers, and administrators is largely the result of the failure of early childhood professionals to clearly articulate what they do and why they do it.

Strategies to inform others about developmentally appropriate practice

All individuals involved in the education of young children—teachers, administrators, and parents—are responsible for ensuring that practices are developmentally appropriate. However, no early childhood professional should abdicate this responsibility in the absence of support from colleagues or supervisors. What can early childhood educators do to fulfill this professional responsibility?

Know what you do and clearly articulate it to others

The lack of understanding about developmentally appropriate practices on the part of many parents, teachers, and administrators is largely the result of the failure of early childhood professionals to clearly articulate what they do and why they do it. Lay-Dopyera and Dopyera (1987) suggest that many early childhood professionals rely on *knowing in action* expertise. Behaviors are carried out almost automatically with little thought to them before or during their performance. These behaviors seem to be natural and we are unaware of where or when they were learned. Perhaps we saw others behaving in this way, noted that it worked,

and adopted these strategies without understanding why. Lay-Dopyera and Dopyera (1987) suggest that early childhood professionals adopt what Donald Schon (1983) calls *reflecting in action.* This means that one pays attention to what one is doing while doing it and thinks about how it is working. Reflecting while teaching helps early childhood professionals to internalize what they do and to explain what they do and why they do it. This book can facilitate the understanding of developmentally appropriate practice, help bring it to consciousness, and assist you in informing others about it. Following are some other suggestions to help adults internalize and convey information about developmentally appropriate practice.

- Read this publication. Use the terminology and definitions as you talk about developmentally appropriate practice.
- Use this publication to assess your own teaching. Identify areas to improve upon and then work on them one at a time.
- Use this publication and other professional materials (position statements from other organizations, articles in educational journals, books) to support your position.
- Join professional organizations. These groups provide teachers with resources; opportunities for professional development such as publications, conferences, meetings, and workshops; and a support system.

85

- Identify other individuals or groups in your community who are working to provide developmentally appropriate experiences for children. If no group exists, start one.
- Identify individuals in leadership positions who support your views and can influence others about inappropriate practice.

Help parents understand developmentally appropriate practice

- Describe your program to parents when children enroll. Provide orientation, parents' meetings, open houses, and parent conferences.
- Use this publication and other professional materials to prepare your presentation and cite your sources. Share these materials with parents.
- Develop a professional library for parents.
- Show a videotape or slides of your classroom demonstrating appropriate practices and explaining the rationale.
- Post signs at each learning center describing the learning that is occurring through developmentally appropriate experiences in that center.
- Mention that you have had specialized training to learn about young children's unique learning styles and appropriate teaching practices.
- Inform parents that you are a member of professional organizations, attend professional meetings, and read current research.
- Send letters or a newsletter to parents describing what children are learning when they work on projects or take field trips.
- Create a parents' bulletin board in or near your classroom, displaying information about and examples of developmentally appropriate practice.
- Use parent volunteers in the classroom. Firsthand experience will promote greater understanding and awareness of developmentally appropriate practice.
- Encourage parent visits. Prepare guidelines telling parents what to look for as they observe active learning.
- Keep a file of children's drawings, writing, artwork, projects, and other products (dated), along with anecdotal records to document and describe development and learning to parents.
- Write articles and take photographs of children engaged in developmentally appropriate projects. Share these with your local newspaper.
- Use the Week of the Young Child and other opportunities to educate parents and the public about developmentally appropriate practice.
- When parents compliment your program, ask them to tell or write your program administrator.

- Develop a network of supportive parents. Involve them with parents who are skeptical of developmentally appropriate practice.
- If a parent asks a question or makes a comment that you do not have time to adequately address, offer to phone them later or to set up a conference after you have had time to organize your thoughts and materials.

Help administrators understand developmentally appropriate practice

Many of the same suggestions mentioned for parents can be used with those in leadership roles in early childhood programs. Following are some additional suggestions.

- Invite your director, supervisor, curriculum consultant, and/or principal to participate in the parent orientation program.
- Ask knowledgeable support personnel to talk with administrators.
- Share textbooks, position statements, and articles from professional journals with administrators.
- Inform your administrator that you are involved in professional organizations, attend professional meetings, and read current research.
- Make administrators honorary members of your local Affiliate Group or other professional groups. Honor them at special meetings for their contributions on behalf of young children.
- Invite administrators to your classroom to participate in activities—reading a story, cooking, or working on a project.
- Share information in a nonthreatening and nondefensive way.
- If an administrator asks a question or makes a seemingly critical comment and you do not have the time to adequately explain, suggest that you have some professional material that you would like to share and schedule a time to discuss the issue more fully.
- Share one or more of the following articles published by the National Association of Elementary School Principals.

Caldwell, B. (1987). The challenge of the third grade slump. *Principal, 66*(5), 10–14.

Cheever, D., & Ryder, A. (1986). Quality: The key to a successful program. *Principal, 65*(6), 18–21.

Elkind, D. (1981). How grown ups help children learn. *Principal, 60*(5), 20–24.

Elkind, D. (1986). In defense of early childhood education. *Principal, 65*(5), 6–9.

Featherstone, H. (1986). Preschool: It does make a difference. *Principal, 65*(5), 16–17.

Fields, M., & Hillstead, D. (1986). Reading begins with scribbling. *Principal, 65*(5), 24–27.

Jennings, G., Burge, S., & Sitek, D. (1987). Half-steps from kindergarten to second grade. *Principal, 66*(5), 22–25.

Kamii, C. (1981). Piaget for principals. *Principal, 60*(5), 8–11.

Nichols, C. (1987). Training new parents to be teachers in rural Missouri. *Principal, 66*(5), 18–21.

Pool, C. (1986). Here come the four-year-olds. *Principal, 65*(5), 4.

Robinson, S. (1987). Are public schools ready for four-year-olds? *Principal, 66*(5), 26–28.

Sava, S. (1985). The right to childhood. *Principal, 64*(5), 56.

Seefeldt, C. (1985). Tomorrow's kindergarten: Pleasure or pressure? *Principal, 64*(5), 12–15.

Zigler, E. (1987). Should four-year-olds be in school? *Principal, 65*(5), 10–15.

Help other teachers understand developmentally appropriate practice

Some of the ideas suggested for increasing parents' and administrator's understanding of developmentally appropriate practice may be used with teachers. Following are some additional ideas.

- Respond calmly to other teachers' seemingly critical remarks. Maintain communcication with colleagues. Discuss your ideas positively and work to continue relationships.
- Informally share information in the teacher's lounge, at lunch, in the office, or before and after the school day.
- Share professional articles, journals, and research with colleagues.

How teacher educators can promote developmentally appropriate practice

- Help students internalize developmentally appropriate practice through course materials and field experiences.
- Prepare students for the "real world." Acquaint them with the reasons parents, administrators, and other teachers may not understand the value of developmentally appropriate practice.
- Provide opportunities for students to demonstrate their ability to communicate about developmentally appropriate practice with others (exams, role play, field experiences, student teaching).
- Provide students with current research documenting the effectiveness of developmentally appropriate practice. Encourage them to maintain a file of such resources.
- Conduct research projects in conjunction with classroom teachers on the short- and long-term effects of appropriate and inappropriate practices on young children.
- Work with teachers during in-service training to promote continuity of developmentally appropriate practices across the full age span of early childhood, birth through age 8.

Help legislators and policymakers understand developmentally apppropriate practice

- Send copies of this publication (or shorter brochures) to key legislators and policymakers, including school board members.
- Share this publication and others about developmentally appropriate practice with key groups such as the local PTA and other educational and professional organizations.
- Write to and meet with policymakers and legislators about the need to provide adequate resources and standards for developmentally appropriate programs. Quote from and reference this book to substantiate your position.

Work with state education administrators and other program administrators

- Know who the decision makers are in your state.
- Establish and maintain contacts and make sure professional organizations have a contact person who keeps members informed.
- Share this publication and other related materials with decision makers.
- Invite state leaders to speak at professional meetings and use public forums to discuss issues of developmentally appropriate practice.

Help publishers and corporations understand developmentally appropriate practice

- Encourage publishers and corporations to hire editors and consultants with training and experience in early childhood development and education.
- Share copies of this book with them.
- Write and thank them if their products are developmentally appropriate.
- Write and explain why a product is developmentally inappropriate. Make suggestions.
- Visit the exhibits at professional meetings. Write letters or give on-the-spot feedback about the appropriateness of exhibitors' products for young children.
- Develop criteria for evaluating products or textbooks that can be used to make curricular decisions for children.

References

Lay-Dopyera, M., & Dopyera, J. (1987). Strategies for teaching. In C. Seefeldt (Ed.), *The early childhood curriculum: A review of research.* New York: Teachers College Press, Columbia University.

Schon, D. (1983). *The reflective practitioner: How professionals think in action.* New York: Basic.

Index

Recess 8, 56
Recordings 4
Redirecting behavior 11, 41, 55
Referrals, to families 13
Relationships. *See* Interaction
Renshaw, P.D. 11, 64
Research 51
Respect
    for children 7–8, 11, 27, 34, 35, 40, 42
    for families 7–8, 12
Responsibilities, for children 4, 12
Rewards 35, 56
Ricciuti, H. 5, 8
Ridicule of children 11
Riley, S.S. 11
Rivkin, M. 3
Rocking chairs 36, 44
Rogers, D.L. 11
Ross, D.D. 11
Rote learning 56
Rubin, K. 11
Rules
    games with 4
    infraction of 11, 55
    moral 65
    rationale for 11
Ruopp, R. 14

-S-
Sackoff, E. 7
Safety 1, 28, 37, 44, 45, 50, 56
Sand 4, 43, 49, 56
Sanders, T. 4
Saracho, O. 7
Schachter, F.F. 10
Schaffer, H.R. 11
Schedule 7, 8, 17, 35, 43, 55
Schickedanz, D.I. 4
Schickedanz, J. 4, 5, 10
Schon, D. 85
School entrance 12–13, 51, 57
Schweinhart, L. 66
Science 4, 54, 56
Scissors 6
Scott, P.M. 11
Screaming, adult 11, 34, 35, 41
Screening 12–13
Seatwork 6, 50, 51
Seefeldt, C. 4
Self-control, achievement of 11, 28, 41, 55
Self-directed play 4
Self-esteem 5, 8, 10, 11, 19, 24, 35, 40, 54
Senses, of children 5, 17–18, 28
Sensorimotor 3, 19
Shaming children 22, 41, 43
Sharing 6, 12, 21, 36, 40, 42
Shure, M.B. 9
Singing 5, 36, 42
Skeen, P. 3, 7
Sleeping 8, 17, 36, 43, 44
Small-group activities 8, 42
Small-motor activities 6, 56
Smith, C.A. 9, 11

Smith, F. 4, 5
Smith, N. 5
Snacks 43, 44
Social development 1–3, 6, 7–8, 9–12, 17–18, 20–21, 24–25, 27–28, 30–31, 40–41, 55
Social studies 56
Souweine, J. 4
Space, arrangement of 36, 44
Sparling, J. 5, 7
Spatial awareness 30–31
Special needs children 4, 13, 57
Spelling 55
Spivak, G. 9
Spodek, B. 3, 7
Sponseller, D. 3
Sprung, B. 7
Staff. *See* Teacher
Standardized tests 12–13, 51, 54, 57
Standards for Educational and Psychological Testing 13
Stern, V. 3, 10, 13
Stewart, I.S. 5, 8, 12
Stipek, D 66
Stone, J.G. 11
Stories 4, 6, 8, 10, 42, 55
Strage, A.A. 10
Stranger anxiety 29
Stress 10, 27, 35
Success, children's feelings of 3, 5, 10, 18, 19, 22, 25, 26–27 *See also* Self-esteem
Supervision 12, 28
Sutton-Smith, B. 3
Sweaney, A.L. 10
Symbolic experiences 4, 6
Szanton, E. 17

-T-
Teacher-directed activity 54, 55
Teacher qualifications 14, 38, 46, 57, 77
Teaching experience 14, 54, 84, 87
Teasing 11, 35
Teberosky, A. 5
Television 35
Testing 12–13, 51, 54, 57, 84
Threatening children 11
3-year-olds 47–50
    adult interaction with 47–50
    as preschoolers 47
    as toddlers 47
    emotional development 47–48
    group care 47, 48
    independence skills 47–48
    language 49
    play 47, 48
    problem solving 49
    social development 48
Tipps, S. 4
Toddlers 17, 21–31
    adult interaction with 9, 22–29, 40–41
    cognitive development 21–24, 28
    competencies 21–24, 30–31, 40–46
    curriculum 5–6, 17–29, 41–44
    daily greeting 41
    emotional development 21–25, 28, 30–31, 40–46

group care iv, 41, 42
    language 5, 9, 22, 25, 31, 40
    physical development 22, 28
    schedule 8, 43
    social development 24–25, 30–31, 40–41
    spatial awareness 31
    See also Dressing, Eating, Toilet learning
Toilet learning 5, 12, 22–24, 29, 41, 43
Torres, R. 66
Toyboxes 37, 45
Toys 4, 5, 28, 37, 40, 45
    battery-powered 37
    realistic 5
    safety of 37
    storage of 37, 45
Trause, M.A. 9
Travers, J. 14
Trost, M. 64
Trust 5, 17, 25
Tull, C. 3, 7

-U-
Uphoff, J.K. 4, 13
U.S. Department of Health and Human Services 60

-V-
Van Deusen-Henkel, J. 63
Veach, D.M. 5, 10, 12
Visitors 12

-W-
Walberg, H. 66
Wallinga, C.R. 10
Warren, R. 10
Water play 4, 11, 20, 28, 43, 49, 56
Waxler, C.Z. 11
Weber, E. 4
Weikart, D. 66
Weissbourd, B. 12, 17
Wellman, H.M. 10
Wells, G. 64
Wheel toys 6
Wilkinson, L. 64
Willert, M. 5
Willfulness 27
Williams, G.A. 64
Willis, A. 5, 8
Wolfgang, C.H. 11
Workbooks 4, 54
Worksheets 4, 22, 56
Writing 4, 6, 55

-Y-
Yarrow, M.R. 11

-Z-
Zavitkovsky, D. 10
Ziegler, P. 12

91

Information about NAEYC,

NAEYC is . . .

. . . a membership supported organization of people committed to fostering the growth and development of children from birth through age 8. Membership is open to all who share a desire to serve and act on behalf of the needs and rights of young children.

NAEYC provides . . .

. . . educational services and resources to adults who work with and for children, including

● *Young Children,* the journal for early childhood educators

● **Books, posters, brochures, and videos** to expand your knowledge and commitment to young children, with topics including infants, curriculum, research, discipline, teacher education, and parent involvement

● An **Annual Conference** that brings people from all over the country to share their expertise and advocate on behalf of children and families

● **Week of the Young Child** celebrations sponsored by NAEYC Affiliate Groups across the country to call public attention to the needs and rights of children and families

● **Insurance plans** for individuals and programs

● **Public affairs information** for informed advocacy efforts at all levels of government and through the media

● The **National Academy of Early Childhood Programs,** a voluntary accreditation system for high quality programs for children

● **The Child Care Information Service,** a computer-based, centralized source of information sharing, distribution, and collaboration.

For free information about membership, publications, or other NAEYC services . . .
. . . call NAEYC at 202-232-8777 or 800-424-2460 or write to

National Association for the Education of Young Children
1834 Connecticut Avenue, N.W., Washington, D.C. 20009-5786